The Business of Drugs

The Business of Drugs

Mary H. Cooper

Washington, D.C. 20037

1414 22nd Street N.W., Washington, D.C. 20037

Printed in the United States of America

Library of Congress Cataloging-in-Publication Data

Cooper, Mary H., 1946—
The business of drugs / Mary H. Cooper.
p. cm.
ISBN 0-87187-499-7
1. Drug traffic. 2. Cocaine industry. 3. Drug abuse--United States.
4. Narcotics, Control of--United States. I. Title.
HV5801.C586 1989
363.4'5'0973--dc20 89-29490
CIP

To my mother and father

Contents

Tables and Figures

TABLES

FIGURES

Preface

It has been called a scourge, the most daunting social problem of the 1980s, even an instrument of genocide aimed against minority communities. Whatever their merits, these and other definitions of drug abuse in the United States apply to an activity whose dynamics are determined by the basic economic law of supply and demand. The business of illicit drugs is fundamentally like any other industry that depends on both ready suppliers and an active market.

Much has been written about the drug epidemic of the 1980s. But most accounts focus on certain aspects of the phenomenon, such as criminal behavior associated with the production and sale of a single substance or the social effects of its use. This book presents a more comprehensive overview of the international business of drugs by concentrating on the economic forces that drive the market. For it is only when these forces are understood that coherent and effective policies to counter the supply and the demand can be formulated. The task is greatly complicated by the illegal nature of the industry itself. Reliable information, especially data showing fluctuations in prices as drugs pass along the distribution chain, is hard to obtain. Further, the links that form that chain are necessarily obscure. Finally, the business of drugs is anything but homogeneous. Patterns of cultivation, production, and early distribution vary greatly from substance to substance. It is not until illegal drugs reach the borders of the United States, the world's leading retail market for illicit drugs, that there is a significant overlap of the trade's various segments.

The industry analysis that makes up the first part of this book is divided into five chapters, each concerned with the cultivation, refinement, and distribution of a single substance or group of similar drugs. Because of growing public concern over the boom in demand for cocaine and its potent derivative, crack, a separate chapter is devoted to the rapidly spreading distribution channels for cocaine within the United States.

The economic forces that drive the illegal drug industry are greatly influenced by federal, state, and local governments' attempts to disrupt them. Chapters 6 through 9 examine both the impact of the business of drugs on American society and the various policy alternatives governments have either considered or adopted to deal with the problem. The late 1980s have seen a renewed campaign to suppress drug abuse by attempting to interrupt the international market forces at play. President Ronald Reagan declared a "war on drugs" and stepped up efforts to interrupt the supply of imported drugs, especially cocaine, into the United States. Congress supported Reagan's campaign and passed increasingly stiff sanctions against the providers and the consumers of illicit drugs. Since succeeding Reagan, George Bush has placed even greater emphasis on the war on drugs and created a new executive position for a "drug czar" to coordinate the activities of numerous federal agencies responsible for fighting the war on several fronts.

Much of the information on the cultivation and production of illegal drugs was compiled from reports published by government offices and agencies. News reports helped bring the book up to date as rapidly unfolding events both in the United States and abroad blurred this snapshot analysis of a diverse, global industry. I wish to thank numerous individuals—both named and unnamed—who provided invaluable information for this volume as well as for an article published in 1988 by Editorial Research Reports, which provided the idea for this book. Unless otherwise noted, citations in the book were based on personal interviews with these sources. I am particularly grateful to Sgt. Pat Moyer and his colleagues of the U.S. Park Police drug enforcement unit in Washington, D.C., for granting me a glimpse of the retail market for illegal drugs in the nation's capital.

Finally, I am grateful to Janet Schilling and Ann O'Malley, who took care of the editing and production of the book, and to Nancy Lammers, who managed the editorial process.

Mary H. Cooper

Introduction
Drugs on the Street: The Last Stop on a Long Journey

The supermarket would not have met public health standards for commercial establishments. Roaches crawled the refrigerator shelves, and the stench of urine filled the air. But the store was well stocked for its purposes. The cabinets contained both new and used 10-mm B&D syringes, a few packets of heroin and cocaine, and Ziploc bags used for packaging marijuana. A small glass pipe used for smoking crack—an increasingly popular and highly addictive form of cocaine—stood in the windowsill.

On the floor, a bare mattress bore evidence that the apartment, a third-floor walk-up in a Washington, D.C., public housing project, was more than a supermarket. It also served as a place to use the goods that were bought there—a "shooting gallery," where anxious heroin consumers could inject their purchases on the spot. Scattered around the rooms were charred bottle caps, used to heat heroin mixed with water, cigarette filters, used to strain impurities from heroin solution as it is drawn into the syringe, and bits of bloody gauze.

Debbie, twenty years old and unemployed, was slumped on a tattered sofa in the living room. Beside her lay a belt, looped through the buckle for use as a tourniquet. Dressed in a gray sweatshirt, gray jogging shorts, and flip-flops, she had come to buy drugs when the police staged the raid. Debbie said she had been shooting heroin for about a year. She bore the sign of her habit—a three-inch long track on her inside right arm below the elbow. She also admitted to smoking cocaine and marijuana, fitting the profile of today's multiple drug user, the "polyaddict." "I used to take loveboat too," she said, referring to a potent and often deadly mixture of marijuana and PCP, "but not since 'boat took my best buddy."

For the police, today's raid was a waste of time. They found no large quantities of illegal drugs, and they made only one arrest among the four people found at the scene, a man who was carrying a small quantity of heroin in his pocket. The establishment's two other employees, near-comatose men who served as lookouts on the steps outside the complex, were released. One had hidden four quarter-gram bags of what appeared to be heroin in his rolled-up sleeves, but chemical analysis proved it to be fake; the man apparently would sell these at the going price of $40 each to other heroin users so that he could return to the store to buy the real thing for himself. Debbie, becoming anxious as the effects of her hit wore off, was also released and hurried away down the street.

The Washington drug outlet, one of hundreds scattered around the capital and one of thousands in other cities across the nation, was only the last link of a long and largely invisible distribution chain along which illegal drugs pass to users in the United States from producers who are often continents away. The multibillion-dollar business of drugs operates in a peculiar economic environment in which the law of supply and demand is often distorted by the illegal nature of the industry. Nevertheless, in many ways, the illegal drug business is like any other business. The consumers, for the most part, are here, in the United States, although Western Europe imports large quantities of heroin, marijuana, and hashish and is becoming a fertile market for South American cocaine. The producers are all over the world, and the industry is made up of distinct sectors, each specializing in a given substance.

1 The Cocaine Oligopoly

Cocaine, because of its increasing popularity in the United States, has been called the drug of the '80s. "There is only one drug for which you can say with certainty that demand has gone up, and that is cocaine," says Peter Reuter, an analyst for the Rand Corporation. "The market for marijuana has been level at best and may actually have declined, and the same is true for heroin. But there is increased demand for high-purity cocaine." Crack, cocaine that can be smoked, has become synonymous with the drug epidemic of the 1980s. Introduced in the early part of the decade, crack is both potent and cheap, selling for as little as $10 a dose. For this reason, it has greater appeal among the young and the poor, particularly vulnerable segments of the population, than the more traditional cocaine powder, which is sniffed. It is also highly addictive. Thanks in part to the sudden increase in demand for crack, the United States accounts for as much as 80 percent of worldwide consumption of cocaine.

Profiting from the new market niche created by the U.S. crack fad is a small group of South American cocaine producers, processors, and exporters who, in little over a decade, have turned the cocaine industry into what may be the most profitable illicit business in history. Cocaine production involves more steps than most illicit drugs. At the same time, of all segments of the illegal drug business, the cocaine industry is the most vertically integrated. "I don't think any organization goes all the way from the plant to the nose," said Rensselaer W. Lee III, president of Global Advisory Services in Alexandria, Virginia, and an expert in the South American illegal drug traffic. "But there is a high level of cooperation among the different organizations that buy coca paste in Peru, turn it into cocaine in Colombia, ship it to the United States and maybe in individual cases are involved in distribution, too."

The crack cocaine sold at neighborhood outlets originates in conditions of poverty perhaps as desperate as those at the retail end. Peasant farmers cultivate the coca bush in remote valleys along the Andes Mountain range, chiefly in Peru, Bolivia, and Colombia, and each producer country occupies a special niche in the initial phase of cocaine production.

Peru

One of the least developed countries in the Western Hemisphere, Peru is the world's leading producer of coca leaves, harvesting enough coca to produce 168 tons of cocaine powder a year. It also is an important source of coca paste and cocaine base, the initial products of the refining process that ends with cocaine powder. Peruvian Indians have traditionally chewed coca leaves to enjoy the mild anesthetic effect they have when broken down by saliva and absorbed in the digestive tract. The government still permits cultivation of up to 18,000 hectares in coca for this purpose. But in 1988, 110,500 hectares were used for coca cultivation, some 80 percent of it illegal.

The Upper Huallaga Valley, a 150-mile-long range of dense jungle along the eastern slopes of the Andes range some 200 miles northeast of Lima, is the center of Peru's $1.2 billion cocaine industry and the world's largest single source of coca leaf. In the valley's marginal rural economy, coca cultivation and paste production may, in Lee's words, "constitute the margin between subsistence and a decent standard of living." As many as 60,000 families are thought to depend on coca growing for their livelihood.[1] More profitable than coffee, bananas, or citrus crops, Peruvian coca bushes can yield four harvests a year and live for fifteen to thirty years in difficult terrain and weather conditions. One hectare can support 10,000-20,000 plants for a yield of 1,000-2,000 kilos of leaves a year. The incentive to cultivate coca for the black market is enhanced by the higher prices traffickers are willing to pay for the dried leaves—$1 a pound compared with 14 cents the same quantity of coca fetches on the legal market.[2]

Even so, the huge harvests of recent years have created a cocaine glut that has pushed down prices, expanding the growers' role in cocaine production. "As the price of leaves has gone down," Lee says, "Peruvian coca growers have found it increasingly desirable to integrate forward into making paste, which they sell to middlemen prior to its export, principally to Colombia." But the Peruvian growers receive only a fraction of 1 percent of the retail earnings from their crop. Because the Peruvian coca growers are disorganized and lack the entrepreneurial leadership of other Latin American producers, the Colombian traffickers were able to gain the dominant role in Peru's cocaine industry.

With U.S. assistance, Peruvian drug-enforcement authorities have destroyed coca fields by manual eradication and have seized clandestine coca-processing laboratories. They have also arrested many people involved in the cocaine trade, more than 7,000 in 1987 alone. But the local police have been less successful in seizing coca paste and cocaine base. Peasants involved in the trade have grown increasingly resistant to the government's antidrug crusade, building their laboratories in more remote and densely wooded areas of the valley to make aerial surveillance more difficult. There they macerate the harvested leaves by stamping on them barefoot. The leaves are soaked in a solvent such as kerosene or bleach, to form coca paste, about 40 percent pure cocaine. This gummy paste is later transformed into cocaine base, which is 90 percent pure cocaine. Stated another way, the typical metric ton harvest of dry leaf from a one-hectare coca plot yields about five kilos of paste, or two kilos of finished cocaine powder.

The chemicals used to transform leaves to coca paste and, in some cases, coca base, are easy to obtain in Peru and throughout the region. Studies conducted in 1987 by the Central Intelligence Agency (CIA) and the Drug Enforcement Agency (DEA) noted a sharp increase in U.S. exports of such "precursor" chemicals as ether and acetone to Latin America. Although these substances have numerous legitimate uses, most of the chemicals found in cocaine labs came from U.S. producers and were diverted from legal export trade to Central and South America.[3]

Drug-enforcement efforts have also been stymied by a growing terrorist presence. In 1984 Sendero Luminoso, or Shining Path, a Maoist guerrilla organization founded in 1970, began expanding its operations from the southern province of Ayacucho into the Upper Huallaga Valley, where the dense foliage provides cover.[4] The organization, which calls for a peasant overthrow of the state, apparently does not participate directly in the cocaine industry; in fact, it condemns the use of drugs and has been known to kill peasants using coca products. But it has found a lucrative source of funds by extracting "taxes" from peasants who grow and process coca for sale to exporters. Shining Path now has virtually complete control over much of the coca cultivation area and has attacked and killed government workers sent in to destroy the crops. With an intensified coca eradication program begun in 1988, more than 5,000 hectares of coca leaf were destroyed that year (Table 1-1). Still, more than 110,000 metric tons of leaf remained available for conversion into cocaine.

Shining Path contributes to the cocaine industry indirectly as well. Like similar groups in other countries of the region, the guerrillas claim to represent the interests of the poor Indian peasantry against the urban ruling class representing the country's white minority. By threatening to overthrow the Peruvian state, Shining Path is diverting government attention and resources away from its coca-eradication program and making it easier for the coca growers to carry on their business. Furthermore, the guerrilla movement appears to be stepping up its activities, profiting from the country's economic crisis.

Peru's economy has grown faster than any other in the region in recent years as wage increases spurred domestic consumption. But domestic production of goods and services has lagged behind the growing demand, aggravating the country's trade imbalance and driving up inflation to more

Table 1-1 South American Cultivation and Eradication of Coca, 1987-1988

	1987		*1988*	
Country	Hectares cultivated	Hectares eradicated	Hectares cultivated	Hectares eradicated
Bolivia	40,300	1,042	49,976	1,476
Colombia	25,000	460	27,230	230
Peru	109,500	355	115,630	5,130
Ecuador	410	110	300	60
Total	175,210	1,967	193,136	6,896

Source: U.S. Department of State, Bureau of International Narcotics Matters, *International Narcotics Control Strategy Report,* March 1989.

than 1,000 percent in 1988. Peru needed increased revenues from exports to service its foreign debt. President Alan Garcia Perez, in an effort to improve the country's economic conditions, introduced an emergency "war economy" plan in March 1988 as the guerrilla movement stepped up its activities in the cities. Price controls and government subsidies were cut, and Garcia announced that certain industries considered vital to the country's welfare, such as food and export goods, would receive government aid.

Until late 1987, Shining Path's guerrillas, who number no more than 3,000-5,000 according to Peruvian government estimates, had limited most of their actions to the countryside. But as peasants have left the mountainous interior in search of work in the cities along the Pacific coast, Shining Path has penetrated the urban areas, including Lima. Terrorist actions on the outskirts of Lima have aroused public indignation and undermine the president's efforts to restore the country's ailing economy. As many as 15,000 people have been killed either by the guerrillas or by the government forces that have been powerless to prevent the group's spread. Human rights advocates claim hundreds more have "disappeared" at the hands of government forces, further undermining the Garcia government's credibility.[5] The navy's land units, made up of urban whites, have been accused of massacring peasants. At the same time, another threat to Peru's governability is the appearance of right-wing paramilitary groups that have claimed responsibility for attacks on public figures.

Bolivia

Although Peru is the world's biggest coca leaf producer, Bolivia, its neighbor to the southeast, is also an important source of coca. The two countries together produce more than 90 percent of the world's coca crop. But the cocaine industry is more tightly organized in Bolivia. Lee calls Bolivia the "grandfather of the cocaine industry," because it is where the business began on a large scale in the late 1970s. It was then that a number of Bolivian families involved in cattle ranching and soybean and sugar farming began to branch out into coca cultivation and processing. At the same time, Lee says, officers of the Bolivian military raided public funds to buy land for cocaine production. "The upper classes of Bolivian society and the military have become coterminous with the cocaine elite in that country," Lee says. He estimates that the Bolivian industry consists of between twelve and twenty-five fairly well integrated family organizations, or mafias, which buy the paste from Peru or from domestic cultivators. About 65 percent of Bolivia's coca cultivation is located in the mountainous Chapare region of Cochabamba Department in the central part of the country. Another important coca-growing region is the Yungas area of La Paz Department. Although favorable soil and climatic conditions permit more efficient use of the land in these regions, Bolivian coca cultivation is only about half the size of Peru's. Bolivia produced an estimated maximum of 67,900 metric tons of coca leaf in 1988, up from 54,961 in 1987.

Like Peru, Bolivia permits the cultivation of small quantities of coca leaf for chewing and for making tea. But these legitimate uses account for only a quarter of the country's coca crop. The Bolivian government has not acted as aggressively as Peru's to curtail illegal coca cultivation. Only 1,000 hectares of coca—out of an estimated 33,000-48,000 hectares used for coca cultivation in Bolivia—were voluntarily eradicated in 1987, the year in which a more stringent narcotics law took effect in that country. In 1988 eradication increased to 1,042 hectares, when even stricter antidrug laws aimed at eliminating all illicit coca cultivation took effect. Under the new laws, Bolivian peasants are to receive $2,000 for every hectare destroyed. The government hoped that this incentive would lure peasants away from coca cultivation, which in recent years has become less profitable for local growers because of overproduction. In 1988 a 100-pound batch of coca leaf fetched only $90 in Bolivia, down from $800 in 1984. Intensified government eradication efforts in 1988 were thought to have pushed prices down further to between $15 and $30 a batch in the main cultivation area of Chapare.[6] Also in 1988, Bolivian authorities arrested and imprisoned Roberto Suarez Gomez, Bolivia's notorious "King of Cocaine," who previously had been sentenced to twelve years in prison for drug smuggling. The Bolivian government rejected a request by the State Department to extradite Suarez to the United States, however, where he is under indictment in Virginia on drug charges.

But it seemed unlikely that these actions would have much effect on the Bolivian cocaine industry, which continues to profit from the country's desperate economic situation. High inflation in the early 1980s eroded workers' earnings and created such chaos that the cocaine industry was able to thrive unimpeded. Widespread corruption of government officials further helped the Bolivian drug producers flourish. By 1985 inflation had soared to 26,000 percent. Under a strict economic austerity program introduced by Victor Paz Estenssoro, who was elected president that year, inflation had fallen to a more tolerable 12 percent by the end of 1988. But Bolivia is still one of the region's poorest countries. The steps taken to reduce inflation, including a tenfold price increase in gas and the closing down of unprofitable state-owned industries, have exacted a heavy toll on the working population. After the collapse of world tin prices in the mid-1980s, the Paz government shut down state-run mines and later dismantled the state-owned mining company COMIBOL, which had employed about 25,000 workers. This action alone left a quarter of the working population jobless.

The collapse of the legitimate economy has left Bolivia with no industry that can generate the employment and income—an estimated $500 million a year—that coca production does. As many as 5 percent of the population, including 42,000 farming families in Chapare, are thought to work for the cocaine industry. In March 1988 some 1,000 former tin miners marched from La Paz to the region of Chulumani seeking work on the region's coca plantations. The peasant farmers of Chulumani reportedly agreed to teach the miners how to grow coca in return for their promise to collaborate in the farmers' campaign to set coca leaf prices.[7]

The Bolivian cocaine mafias control the rural laboratories where coca leaf is processed into paste and 90 percent pure cocaine base, which they sell to exporters. Several organizations have managed to establish trafficking links to the United States via Mexico, but most of their control ends at the Bolivian border. The Bolivians sell some cocaine paste and base to smugglers in Brazil, where they obtain most of the chemicals used to process coca. Some of them, Lee says, take the process one step further and transform base into cocaine hydrochloride, or powder, an equally pure form of the drug, and ship it directly to the U.S. or Western European market. But most Bolivian coca paste and base is sold to the Colombians, who dominate the downstream activities of the cocaine industry.

Although political and economic conditions in Peru and Bolivia differ, cocaine profits make an important contribution to the overall economies of both countries. "The traditional Andean commodities are down," Lee says, "and this makes cocaine exports more important." Although most of the profits from the cocaine industry are invested in U.S. stocks and real estate or secreted in offshore tax havens such as the Cayman Islands and Panama, the repatriated "narcodollars" contribute greatly to these countries' ailing economies. According to Lee's analysis, repatriated earnings from cocaine exports equal 20 to 30 percent of Peru's legal exports and between 50 and 100 percent of Bolivia's. Much of the money, of course, does not benefit the general population. Cocaine traffickers in both countries use much of the profit to invest in clandestine airstrips, chemicals, and labor inherent to the trade. A large amount of the earnings also are used to bribe government officials, to pay "taxes" to guerrilla organizations that control areas of coca cultivation, and to buy weapons used by security forces guarding coca transport routes. Even when industry profits do return to the local economy, they are not always invested efficiently. Lee describes the "schizophrenic development" that has taken place in the "coca boom towns" of Peru's Upper Huallaga Valley. Although one such town still has no sewage system, drinking water, or paved roads, it boasts "six banks, six Telex machines, several stereo dealerships, and one of the largest Nissan outlets in Peru." [8]

But not all the repatriated narcodollars are squandered. The Bolivian cocaine mafia, Lee says, invests heavily in its members' traditional ranching economy, improving livestock and such legal crops as cotton and sugar cane. Before his arrest in July 1988, Suarez is said to have restored buildings, built roads, and provided scholarships for poor students in his native region of Beni. He and the other participants in Bolivia's cocaine trade repatriated $486 million a year in the mid-1980s to spend in public works projects as a way to win popular support for their business.

In addition to such direct investments, the cocaine trade provides a vital stimulus to the economy. Lee estimates that the Peruvian economy gains $700 million a year from cocaine sales. In view of the collapse in the world price of oil, one of the country's main salable commodities, cocaine is now "by far Peru's most important export." Although Bolivia earns less in drug profits—some $250-$450 million, Lee estimates—the crash in international prices for Bolivian tin and natural gas has enhanced cocaine's role as the leading generator of foreign exchange for that country as well. The third world debt crisis has further reduced alternative sources of income for these countries: Peru, for example, owes foreign lenders almost $300 million. "Neither Peru nor Bolivia can get commercial loans," Lee says, "and Peru can't get loans from anyone."

With U.S. material and financial aid, the producing countries' governments have attempted to destroy crops by manual eradication and aerial spraying. But their efforts have not curtailed coca production. In fact, quite the opposite is the case. The State Department's Bureau of International Narcotics Matters estimates that Andean coca production is increasing by 5 to 10 percent a year. Led by Peru, where coca production jumped from 95,000 metric tons in 1985 to as much as 124,000 metric tons in 1988, the region's coca growers were expected to harvest up to 230,000 metric tons in 1989 (Table 1-2).

But as profitable as the drug trade is, Lee points out, it is an inefficient generator of wealth for these poor producer countries. In the first place, most of the profits are invested in foreign economies, either as bank deposits or as direct business investments. What profits return to the producer country are by their illicit nature not subject to taxation and thus never find their way into public investment that might improve the standard of living. Much of the repatriated drug money is spent by the producers themselves to bribe politicians, judges, police officials, and other authorities not to interfere with the drug trade. What money the drug lords do spend to improve living conditions—constructing new apartment buildings and schools, for example—tends to be highly localized and benefits only the townspeople in the producers' bases of operations. In any event, these expenditures can be regarded as business overhead, investments to ensure the cooperation of authorities and the public support needed to continue operations. Because coca is by far the most lucrative crop available to peasants, its cultivation also may curtail the production of traditional food crops, raising the market prices of consumer staples.

Coca cultivation is also fast destroying the producer countries' capacity to produce legal crops. In the decade since the cocaine industry took off, the clearing of huge tracts of forested and often steeply sloping land for coca planting has aggravated soil erosion. The heavy use of chemical fertilizers in the coca fields as well as toxic chemicals such as acetone, kerosene, quicklime, sulfuric acid, and toluene used in the processing pits are polluting ground water and surface water supplies. At least 150 rivers in the Upper Huallaga Valley have been poisoned, possibly irreparably, according to Peruvian scientists.[9] "When the sun hits the Huallaga River at just the right angle, the chemical pollution—a yellow color—can be seen from the air," said former secretary of state George Shultz after a tour of the region. "That's the color of a dying land."[10]

But the cocaine industry also provides general economic benefits that in part explain its success in the producer countries. Bolivia and Peru, the poorest of the three main cocaine producers, have perhaps the most to gain from the drug trade. Both countries have long depended on the export of tin, copper, natural gas, and oil for foreign exchange. World prices for these commodities plummeted in the first half of the 1980s, drastically reducing the two countries' income from foreign trade at a time when the third world debt crisis had virtually eliminated sources of borrowed money from the United States and other industrial nations. Unable to pay off their foreign loans, Bolivia and Peru also faced domestic unrest as mines and oil fields laid off workers.

Cocaine is the only major Andean commodity whose foreign demand has risen in the 1980s. The cocaine industry has provided an effective buffer against job losses in other export-dependent industries. When world prices for Bolivian tin fell below the cost of extracting it in 1986, mines closed and more than 20,000 Bolivian tin miners were out of work. As many as 5,000 of them, Lee estimates, left the coastal mining areas and moved to the highlands to seek work in the coca fields. A Bolivian government document Lee cites, the "Triennial Program for the Battle against Drug Trafficking," provides evidence of the cocaine industry's ability to compensate for inadequacies in the legal economy. From 1980 to 1986, as the country's total output of goods and services (gross national product) fell by 16 percent, coca production increased by an estimated 35 percent.

The drug industry's ability to absorb jobless workers is even more impressive: the government document reported that while official unemployment more than tripled over the first six years of the decade, from 5.7 percent to 20 percent, so did the number of families cultivating coca. Lee estimates that some half million people in the Andean region, mostly in Bolivia and Peru, earn their livelihoods by growing and harvesting coca leaves. Hundreds of thousands more work in successive stages of the drug's production and export. Many are involved directly with the production process, macerating leaves or refining paste into powder. Others work on the construction of clandestine laboratories and airstrips, which can be a full-time occupation when government crackdown efforts are at a peak. Still others act as security personnel, guarding the trails that link the coca fields with processing labs. Middlemen carry on a lucrative trade, buying and selling leaves, paste, or powder to others who then smuggle the product to neighboring countries. Altogether, Lee estimates, 350,000 to 400,000 people in Bolivia alone—5 to 6 percent of the population—are directly employed in the cocaine industry. And this figure excludes those who profit indirectly from the illegal trade by selling goods and services to the cultivators and traffickers. So vast is the Andean economy's dependence on the cocaine industry, Lee says, that "if the industry were shut down tomorrow, economic and political chaos would reign in Bolivia and Peru and possibly in Colombia as well."

Colombia

Compared with Peru and Bolivia, Colombia is an economic success story. As its neighbors stood on the brink of bankruptcy, Colombia's economy grew steadily in the 1980s, by 5.5 percent in 1987 alone. Although Colombia also borrowed heavily in the 1970s and currently owes about $19 billion to international lenders, it is one of the few third world borrowers that has kept up with its debt repayments. As profitable as coca cultivation and processing are to the producers, they pale in comparison with the profit-making potential of exporting cocaine powder. It is this stage of the cocaine business that is dominated by a group of between five and ten

Colombian organizations, the biggest of which is the Medellin cartel, named after the country's second-largest city, where it is based. The only other organization powerful enough to warrant the title cartel is based in Cali, Colombia's third-largest city. Together, the cartels control about 90 percent of the world's cocaine business.

Organizations in other countries are also involved in cocaine export. As law-enforcement efforts have succeeded in intercepting some shipments into the United States by way of Florida, traffickers based in Mexico are gaining a foothold in the business by transporting cocaine into the lucrative North American market by land and air over the long and sparsely populated U.S.-Mexican border. At least a third of the cocaine sold in the United States enters the country from Mexico, more than from any other country. Since 1983, the Mexican government claims to have seized almost 50,000 pounds of cocaine headed for the United States with a street value of more than $20 billion. But there is evidence that this shift in trafficking patterns was also the work of Colombia's drug lords, who have established ties with forces in Panama, Nicaragua, and Honduras. They also have gained footholds in Jamaica, the Bahamas, Cuba, Haiti, and other Caribbean islands that serve as convenient intermediate points for cocaine destined for the North American market. Indeed, the Colombian organizations have held on to their dominant market share throughout the cocaine boom of the 1980s. In Lee's view, the reason is simple. "These Colombians come out of a tradition that is quite exceptional for Latin American culture," he said. "They are modernizers and tremendously good businessmen who come out of an entrepreneurial tradition."

Like its smaller competitors, the Medellin cartel is a relatively new organization that came into being in the late 1970s with the rise in demand for cocaine in North America. At first, cocaine producers relied on small crops grown by Indians in southwestern Colombia. Exports were limited to small packages smuggled on commercial airline flights into the United States. As demand for cocaine overtook the Colombian growers' ability to harvest coca leaf, the exporters began to refine paste they bought from Bolivian growers.

By some accounts, the highly organized drug mafia that exists in Colombia today owes its success largely to the dreams of one man, Carlos Enrique Lehder Rivas. While serving time in a U.S. prison for marijuana smuggling, Lehder is said to have laid out his plan to consolidate Colombia's fragmented cocaine exporting business. Lehder's plan involved smuggling massive shipments of cocaine to the United States aboard private airplanes in order to make the export business more efficient. After his release from prison in the mid-1970s, Lehder began collaborating with Jorge Luis Ochoa Vasquez, a leader in the existing cocaine-smuggling operations headquartered in Medellin.[11]

Today, the Colombian cartels are based in Medellin and Cali. Lee estimates that the cartels control about 80 percent of the country's cocaine powder exports and 60 percent of the cocaine sold in the United States. The rest of the Colombian cocaine trade is thought to be controlled by small refiners, many of whom are allied with FARC (Revolutionary Armed Forces of Colombia), one of several local guerrilla organizations. FARC does not appear to share Shining Path's abhorrence of drug use and may control some coca paste laboratories in the remote southeastern part of the country where the group's peasant supporters also grow coca leaf for sale to the cartel.

Relations between the drug lords and Colombia's four main guerrilla organizations are a matter of controversy. Some observers, including officials of the Reagan administration, have warned that an emerging alliance between cocaine traffickers and guerrilla organizations threatens to bring down what remains of Colombia's civilian government. In 1984, after Lewis Tambs, then U.S. ambassador to Colombia, suggested the connection, U.S. officials have repeatedly warned of a conspiracy between drug traffickers and rebel groups aimed at orchestrating "narcoguerrilla" takeovers of Colombia and other countries involved in the drug trade. Even the prestigious Institute for Strategic Studies in London, considered the most authoritative nongovernmental source of information on world armaments, has ranked "narcoterrorism" with communism as one of the two greatest threats to Western interests in the region.[12]

Supporters of the narcoterrorist theory point to an incident in November 1985. The Medellin cartel reportedly paid the "March 19 Movement," or M-19, between $1 million and $5 million to take over the Palace of Justice and hold hostage the Supreme Court justices in an effort to persuade them not to extradite cartel members to the United States for trial. In the resulting shootout with government troops, nearly one hundred persons, including eleven justices, died.

But other evidence suggests that such dealings are not aimed at establishing a lasting political alliance. For one thing, the *narcotraficantes* are quintessential capitalists and show little taste for many of the groups' revolutionary goals. While their ideologies, national aims, and emphasis on urban or rural development differ, guerrilla organizations in the three main cocaine-producing nations share a goal of destroying the capitalist social and economic order. It is hard to imagine why the *narcotraficantes*, with their evident taste for conspicuous consumption and personal gain, would undermine the very system that allows them to prosper.

In fact, the Medellin cartel originated in a coordinated attack by cocaine traffickers against M-19. The guerrilla organization, which has grown since its founding in 1970 to include between 500 and several thousand members, frequently funds its operations with ransom money extorted from the families of its kidnap victims. But in 1981, when the guerrillas kidnapped the daughter of Fabio Ochoa Restrepo, a Medellin capo, and demanded $12 million in ransom, the cocaine exporters formed a small army of security forces to bring to a halt M-19's tactic of extortion by kidnapping. The same year they also agreed to collaborate in the cocaine-refining process, setting the stage for closer coordination of their activities.

The name of the cartel's antikidnapping force—"Death to the Kidnappers" *(Muerte a Los Secuestradores,* or MAS)—hardly suggests the likelihood of an alliance between cocaine traders and guerrillas. In fact, its creation marked the beginning of the series of killings of both peasants and public officials that continues to this day. In addition, MAS pushed the coca growers allied with FARC out of large areas of the country.[13] "The goals of the guerrillas and the traffickers are fundamentally incompatible," writes Bruce Bagley, a professor of international studies at the University of Miami. "The guerrillas are revolutionaries who seek to overthrow the Colombian system; the traffickers are robber-baron capitalists who seek to protect their ill-gotten gains and assure themselves immunity from prosecution. Their stormy relations have involved far more bloodshed than cooperation."[14]

M-19 and the *narcotraficantes* do appear to have established an occasional working relationship, by which the guerrillas refrain from kidnapping family members of cocaine dealers and collaborate in assassination attempts against public officials who threaten the cocaine lords' business, such as the 1985 siege against the Palace of Justice. But such arrangements appear to be purely opportunistic. Members of other leftist groups, including FARC, have been targeted for assassination by the drug lords, apparently because they promise to institute land reform if they gain power. The cartel members, who have bought vast tracts of land with their profits from the cocaine trade, are adamantly opposed to any scheme that would redistribute land to the country's peasant farmers.

Greater danger to the civilian governments of the region may come from right-wing paramilitary groups. If a change in the existing order is to be made, the drug lords might have more to gain from the rise to power in the main cocaine-producing countries of traditional military juntas than from revolution on the left. Latin American military dictatorships have traditionally enlisted the support of domestic business leaders and landowners as guarantors of the status quo and as protection from nationalization and land reform, frequent goals of the region's parties of the left. Some observers believe that the threat of right-wing takeover is becoming increasingly evident in Colombia.[15] If the traffickers supported such a military coup, they could gain the legitimacy they seek, not in least part to reduce the enormous overhead that now goes to paying private security forces and bribing government officials. Such an alliance would not be new to the region. Roberto Suarez Gomez enjoyed freedom to run his cocaine business after Gen. Luis Garcia Meza staged his coup in Bolivia in 1980 and appointed Suarez's nephew minister of the interior.

These small producers are dwarfed, however, by the tightly controlled Medellin cartel. Lee estimates that the organization is directed by about 100 people under the leadership of eight men. Five of them are based in Medellin: Pablo Emilio Escobar Gaviria, Jose Gonzalo Rodriguez Gacha, and three Ochoa Vasquez brothers, Jorge Luis, Juan David, and Fabio. The other three leaders—Gilberto Jose Rodriguez, Miguel Angel Rodriguez Orjuela, and Jose Santacruz Londono—are based in Cali. Like many large legitimate corporations, the Medellin cartel is divided into divisions. Escobar, who acts as the cartel's acknowledged chairman and chief executive officer, also heads the security side of business, running two training centers for his 200-man army. Jorge Ochoa, Escobar's deputy, and his brothers are said to oversee the cocaine distribution networks in Florida and California. Rodriguez, Rodriguez Orjuela, and Santacruz run the networks in New York City and Houston from their headquarters in Cali. Reuter of the Rand Corporation compares these drug lords with the heads of a medium-size corporation. "I don't know that they are involved in anything terribly different," he said. "Instead of lobbying, they make direct payments to public officials to get what they want from government."

Lee places the value of the entire South American cocaine trade at as much as $4 billion per year, of which $3 billion is accounted for by Colombia alone. Cocaine has even overtaken coffee as Colombia's most lucrative export. The Medellin cartel, in turn, controls an estimated 80 percent of the Colombian industry, for annual earnings of $2.4 billion. The country's drug lords have become fabulously wealthy: By 1987, Jorge Ochoa and Pablo Escobar had even made *Forbes* magazine's list of the world's billionaires. The cartel has often been called a state within a state, and its political clout suggests that the term is well-earned. In 1984 the cartel reportedly offered to pay off the country's $9 billion external debt if the Colombian government would scrap an extradition treaty with the United States and drop all criminal charges against the cartel's leaders. More recently, in July 1988, a Senate Foreign Relations subcommittee heard evidence of the cartel's growing power throughout the Southern Hemisphere. The cartel is said to have tried to buy $4 million worth of missiles and other weapons from arms dealers. According to testimony, the cartel leadership also attempted in 1986 to negotiate a kind of international treaty with the U.S. government, under which the drug lords would agree to stop selling drugs to the United States and provide information on Colombia's guerrilla organizations in exchange for amnesty from extradition and prosecution.[16] The State Department declined the offer.

But the Colombian drug lords do not have full control over their industry. Like OPEC, whose attempts to control the production and price of oil have declined in recent years, the Medellin cartel does not have the power to set cocaine prices or limit its production. While it has been highly successful in meeting the growing demand for cocaine in North America by streamlining its smuggling activities, the cartel has been powerless to stop the slide in the drug's wholesale price, from $60,000 a kilo in 1980 to less than $10,000 in 1987.[17] The cartel's main function, Reuter said, is to coordinate the activities and share the costs of the cocaine export business, especially those derived from the illegal nature of the business. "It is cheaper for five of them to buy a colonel [together] than for each one to buy him separately." In addition, Lee said, the cartel members enter into joint ventures with one another and occasionally share inventory: "If the Ochoa family doesn't have enough cocaine on hand to satisfy the need of a customer, they will borrow cocaine from the Escobar organization."

The cartel's hold over the cocaine industry begins in Peru's Upper Huallaga Valley, where Colombian agents act as middlemen to purchase paste for later refining or as mercenaries to guard shipments on their way to Colombia. There, the cartel controls most of the final processing into cocaine powder and the product's export to the United States. Peru and Bolivia together account for the bulk of Colombia's raw material. What portion of it has not already been processed into powder in the country of origin is refined in Colombia before export. As demand for cocaine has risen, however, the Colombians have also invested more heavily in coca cultivation at home, transforming Colombia into the world's third biggest coca producer.

Cocaine export is a highly specialized segment of the industry, requiring an extensive network of alternative transportation routes and shipment modes to evade detection by law-enforcement authorities along the way to market. In accordance with Lehder's prescription, cocaine destined for southern Florida, the main point of entry into the United States, and New York, the next most common port, is usually shipped in bundles of several hundred kilos, most often in general aviation aircraft and, slightly less frequently, aboard noncommercial vessels. The cartel has invested heavily in sophisticated aircraft and boats. Cocaine transport planes often are equipped with electronic navigation equipment that allows pilots to fly close to the ground and thus escape radar detection while entering U.S. air space. The Medellin cartel's efforts to streamline its export operations are paying off. Between 1976, about the time Lehder returned to Colombia, and 1982, cocaine exports to the United States grew from an estimated 14-19 metric tons to 45 metric tons.

Although pilots occasionally fit extra fuel tanks into their planes' unused storage areas in order to make the trip nonstop, Colombia's distance from the United States (about 1,500 miles) makes it hard for small aircraft to reach their destination without refueling. The exporters' shipping costs, therefore, must include bribes of government officials to permit fueling stopovers in countries along the way—Panama, Mexico, and especially the Bahamas, Haiti, and other island nations of the Caribbean. Several of the Medellin cartel's mid-level drug lords who have stood trial or been imprisoned in the United States, such as Lehder and Juan Ramon Matta Ballesteros, have been involved mainly in these downstream activities. Lehder, who in 1988 was again sent to jail, this time to life in prison for importing 3.3 tons of cocaine into the United States, acted as what Lee calls an "expediter" who provided a transit point for Colombian cocaine headed for the United States. Until his arrest in Medellin in 1987, Lehder directed a fleet of private aircraft on Norman's Cay, his island in the Bahamas, that received shipments from Colombia and carried them on to their destination points in the United States. Matta, too, appears not to have been involved directly in cocaine production but rather to have served as what Lee called an "international representative or trouble-shooter" for the Colombian exporters from his bases in Honduras and elsewhere.

While the cocaine industry yields huge profits, Colombian society is paying a heavy price for the country's booming drug business. The gap between rich and poor in Colombia is among the widest in the region. Although the country has been under civilian rule for the past thirty years, it is virtually ungovernable, as various guerrilla organizations vie with *narcotraficantes* for control. Many Colombians have paid for this struggle with their lives: More than 16,000 Colombians were murdered in 1987, a 15 percent increase over the year before. Many were slain by guerrillas; at least eight guerrilla groups of the left and right are active in Colombia. But political assassinations, which have long been common in Colombia, may now be outnumbered by drug-related killings. Although cartel members cooperate among themselves at various stages in the distribution network, they also compete for dominance of the trade. The drug lords hire assassins known as *sicarios* to kill rival traffickers and their workers.

Industry magnates have not hesitated to assassinate government officials who have stood in their way, especially those who refuse to block the extradition of cartel members to the United States, where many are wanted on drug trafficking charges. In Colombia alone, more than 200 judges and court employees, a newspaper editor, and numerous other public figures—not to mention more than 400 police and military personnel—have paid with their lives for impeding the cartel's operations. Over a three-day period in August 1989, a judge, a provincial police chief, and a popular senator who had been expected to win the 1990 presidential election were assassinated. Because all three victims were outspoken critics of the cocaine trade, the assassinations were seen as the work of the drug lords. Until the murders of August 1989, the most blatant use of assassination to influence policy was the 1984 killing of Rodrigo Lara Bonilla, a minister of justice. Lara was responsible for a raid on the cartel's main cocaine-refining lab that resulted in the biggest cocaine seizure on record, worth $1.2 billion. Barely a month later, he was murdered in downtown Bogota. Like the recent killings, Lara's assassination provoked an uproar in Colombia and prompted the government to crack down on the cocaine trade. Belisario Betancur Cuartas, Colombia's president at the time, ordered the extradition of some twenty suspected cocaine dealers to the United States. Cartel leaders fled to Panama, where they reportedly paid military strongman Gen. Manuel Antonio Noriega between $4 million and $5 million to grant them refuge.[18] But the crackdown produced only a temporary setback in the cartel's fortunes. In June 1987 the Colombian Supreme Court succumbed to the cartel's pressure and suspended the 1979 extradition treaty with the United States.

Colombia's current president, Virgilio Barco Vargas, who succeeded Betancur in 1986, agrees with outside observers that the cocaine industry is a major threat to his country's democratic institutions. In January 1988, shortly after his attorney general, Carlos Mauro Hoyos Jimenez, was assassinated in Medellin, Barco launched a new antidrug program called the "Decree for the Defense of Democracy." The new laws called for thirty-year prison sentences for anyone who kills a policeman, longer terms for anyone engaging in terrorism, and three to six years for making death threats. In a bid to lure judges and prosecutors to take on drug cases—an undertaking that has cost numerous Colombian jurists their lives—the government promised to buy up to $37,000 in life insurance for those who participate in trials of accused drug dealers. Barco responded even more forcefully to the 1989 assassination of presidential candidate Luis Carlos Galan by arresting 11,000 suspected drug traffickers and confiscating ranches, weapons, and other assets worth more than $125 million. Far more threatening to the cartel leaders, none of whom were found in the police sweep, was Barco's announcement August 17 that he would bypass the beleaguered judicial system and extradite cartel leaders to the United States where they are wanted on felony drug charges. In response to the government's antidrug campaign, the cocaine traffickers issued a declaration of "total war" against all who support their extradition.

As the cocaine industry has emerged as Colombia's chief generator of foreign exchange, its leaders have gained leverage in the country's political life by more subtle means. Cocaine magnates have purchased newspapers and radio stations, they campaign actively on issues that affect the industry, and they give financial support to candidates for public office who promise to be tolerant of the illegal drug industry. Escobar himself stood for office in 1982 and was elected as an alternate congressman for his home district.

The cartel has further strengthened its control over public opinion by making conspicuous investments in popular initiatives that the legitimate government can ill afford. Lee cites the example of Jose Gonzalo Rodriguez Gacha, who, in addition to providing employment and raising the salaries of the inhabitants of his home town near Bogota, has built an outdoor basketball court and rebuilt the town hall's facade with his drug earnings. Likewise, Pablo Escobar has built soccer fields and a 500-unit housing project in Medellin and is famous for his gifts to the poor. "Escobar is viewed as something close to a deity there," Lee said. "Nobody speaks ill of that guy in Medellin. Nobody."

Like the major coca-producing countries, Colombia and other exporting nations derive considerable economic benefits from the cocaine trade. Lee calculates that the $300-$500 million in profits from the cocaine industry that are repatriated to Colombia each year place it among the top three leading export businesses in the country, together with coffee and oil, even though that sum is a minuscule portion of the illegal drug profits. About $12 billion in Colombian drug earnings, Lee estimates, remain in the United States, where the money is "laundered" and funneled into such licit investments as stocks, bonds, real estate, and Treasury bills.

Billions more narcodollars are thought to be deposited in the Cayman Islands, Panama, and other countries whose bank secrecy laws prevent their seizure by drug-enforcement authorities. Earnings from cocaine sales in the United States are pooled in "safe houses" in the major cocaine retail centers of New York, Chicago, Los Angeles, San Francisco, Dallas, Houston, and New Orleans. The cash is packaged and shipped to foreign banks. Panama, which uses the U.S. dollar as its currency, remains the chief Latin American financial center for narcodollars. General Noriega was indicted in February 1988 on drug trafficking and drug-money laundering charges by federal grand juries in Tampa and Miami. According to the indictment, the money is received by government troops and trucked to the National Bank of Panama. There the money is deposited into accounts held by dummy corporations that are registered to do business in the United States. The drug proceeds can then be used to make legitimate investments both in the United States and elsewhere.[19]

President Barco's extradition decree of August 1989 seemed likely to bring some cartel leaders to justice in the United States. But it remains to be seen how recent arrests of Colombian cocaine traffickers will affect the Medellin cartel's business. Carlos Lehder's 1988 imprisonment in the United States has had no apparent effects on the flow of cocaine into the country.

The cheapest but riskiest means of transporting finished cocaine from Colombia to North America is the commercial airliner. Much of the cocaine is smuggled directly on regularly scheduled commercial flights. U.S. drug-enforcement agents have made at least fourteen seizures of cocaine aboard airplanes of Avianca Airlines, Colombia's national airline. Only relatively small quantities of cocaine can be shipped in a single load, however. Larger shipments can be sent in seagoing cargo vessels, but these are slow and, like commercial aircraft, subject to scrutiny by customs officials.

Increasingly, the preferred mode of shipment is the general aviation aircraft, which, when gutted of inessential equipment, can carry large loads of cocaine. Outfitted with radar-detection devices and manned by well-paid expert pilots, these small private planes can land in any number of remote fields or country roads in the southern United States, unload their cargo, and leave the country again within minutes without ever being detected. But because of the distances involved, these aircraft must stop to refuel or transfer cargo to other planes somewhere between Colombia and the United States.

For this reason, an essential component of the cocaine industry's operations is the maintenance of reliable stopover points between production facilities in northwestern South America and the main distribution points in North America. Cocaine trafficking is banned in the countries of Central America and the Caribbean that lie along the route, so a good deal of the cartel's overhead expenses consist in bribes of government officials outside Colombia. Many islands in the Caribbean close to Florida, such as the Bimini Islands and the Bahamas, serve as the last stop for cocaine headed to the United States. At least half the cocaine that enters this country is thought to pass through the Bahamas. It is widely alleged that Carlos Lehder, who initially directed the cartel's shipment routes, paid the government of Bahamian prime minister Sir Lynden O. Pindling to ignore the frequent flights into and out of Lehder's island in the Bahamas, less than 100 miles off the Florida coast. According to evidence presented at Lehder's trial in Jacksonville, Pindling himself received hundreds of thousands of dollars from Lehder's trafficking operation.

Similar arrangements are said to have been made in Mexico, whose 2,000-mile land border with the United States has made the country an attractive route for cocaine smugglers. Directing these operations are several drug rings, the strongest of which is headed by Rafael Caro Quintero and based in the state of Sonora, a desert region in the northwestern corner of Mexico across the border from Arizona. As part of the arrangement, Colombian dealers trade cocaine for weapons Caro Quintero's agents smuggle from the United States. After the 1985 torture and death in Mexico of Enrique Camarena Salazar, an agent of the U.S. Drug Enforcement Agency, charges of government corruption mounted. Caro Quintero, a prime suspect in the Camarena murder, is serving a thirty-four-year sentence on unrelated drug charges in a Mexico City prison, from which he allegedly continues to direct his smuggling operations. Under pressure from U.S. allegations of lax treatment of drug traffickers, President Carlos Salinas de Gortari took office in December 1988 with a pledge to step up drug-enforcement efforts. The Salinas government fulfilled its promise in April 1989 by arresting another leading cocaine smuggler, Miguel Angel Felix Gallardo.

Other Countries Involved in the Cocaine Trade

The cocaine industry has spread beyond its base in Peru, Bolivia, and Colombia. After the Colombian government cracked down on the drug trade and forced the cartel leaders into exile, they decided to expand their base of operations. The drug lords stepped up their efforts in the mid-1980s, when drug-enforcement authorities throughout the region and in the United States intensified the interdiction of cocaine shipments through traditional routes in the Caribbean. At the same time, the American cocaine habit was spreading rapidly to Western Europe. Like any good corporate board of directors, the cartel leaders decided to spread their risks and expand their market outlets to satisfy growing demand for their product. They did not have far to look.

Because the demand for cocaine has risen in recent years in Europe, the drug lords turned to Brazil, with its closer proximity to the European continent than Colombia, Peru, and Bolivia and to the cartel's established transshipment points in the Caribbean and Mexico. Because of the recent oversupply of cocaine and consequent fall in prices for the drug in the United States, cocaine fetches a higher price in many European markets, which have not yet been affected by the glut. Rio de Janeiro, Brazil's largest city and a major commercial airline hub linking South America with both North America and Western Europe, was an ideal candidate. The country trades heavily with both regions, presenting considerable opportunity for smuggling cocaine in shipments of legal goods.

Brazil presents other advantages as well. South America's largest nation, Brazil shares land borders with all three major cocaine producers along a 4,000-mile stretch of mostly remote territory. Couriers, known as "mules," carry coca paste and refined cocaine powder overland from all three producer countries into Brazil with little fear of detection by authorities. Larger quantities are shipped in by air. The Amazon River and its tributaries that reach into Colombia, Peru, and Bolivia also offer convenient routes for transporting cocaine across the continent to the Atlantic and beyond. Authorities in Tampa, Florida, recently seized cocaine that had been hidden in a shipment of cedar board and transported along the Amazon.[20]

Like its neighbors that produce coca leaf, Brazil offers a hospitable environment for cocaine-processing laboratories. The country's vast unde-

Table 1-2 South American Production of Coca (in thousands of metric tons), 1985-1989

Country	1985	1986	1987	1988	1989
Bolivia	42.0-53.2	44.0-52.9	46.0-67.0	57.4-78.4	58.4-79.6
Colombia	12.4	12.0-13.6	18.0-23.0	19.0-24.2	19.0-24.2
Peru	95.2	95.0-120.0	98.0-121.0	97.0-124.0	98.4-125.9
Ecuador	1.9	1.0	.4	.3-.5	.2-.3
Total	151.5-162.7	152.0-187.5	162.4-211.4	173.7-227.1	176.0-229.9

Source: U.S. Department of State, Bureau of International Narcotics Matters, *International Narcotics Control Strategy Report*, March 1989.

veloped spaces stretching hundreds of miles west of the Atlantic coast include dense jungle that lends itself to clandestine activities from coca cultivation to refining. Coca plantations have sprung up in northwestern Brazil where tributaries of the Amazon River offer transportation links to neighboring Colombia. And unlike the traditional Andean coca-growing nations, Brazil offers the convenience of an established chemicals industry, which produces some of the precursor chemicals that are needed to turn coca paste into cocaine powder. Thus the Brazilian labs do not have to smuggle acetone and ether into the country but can buy these chemicals domestically.

The Colombian drug lords have received an extra bonus from expanding their business into Brazil in Rio itself, which has become an important retail market. Most of the city's nine million inhabitants live in poverty, scattered in shantytowns that line the slopes of the steep hills surrounding the city. Slum youths sell the Colombians' product to their neighbors and enjoy a free hand to control their territories. Dozens of slum areas are controlled by these heavily armed cocaine retailers. Like the Colombian drug lords, Rio's cocaine traffickers often are seen as allies by the slum dwellers in their struggle against poverty many consider imposed by the state. In contrast to the authorities, who stage periodic raids to oust squatters in the city's teeming outskirts, the cocaine dealers hand out food and money, provide jobs, and act as mediators in local disputes.[21]

Brazil is the biggest new participant in the South American cocaine trade, but neighboring countries outside the traditional cocaine-producing region are also becoming involved. The government of Ecuador apparently succeeded in eliminating coca cultivation in the mid-1980s, but remains an important crossroads for the traffic of cocaine headed to U.S. markets and of precursor chemicals destined for processing labs in Colombia and elsewhere. Like Brazil, Venezuela and Argentina have become important transit points for Colombian cocaine destined for North America and Europe. Venezuela's sparsely populated border with Colombia provides a convenient conduit for the cartel's shipments out of the region. DEA estimates that some fifteen tons of cocaine were shipped through Venezuela in 1988, almost four times the amount recorded in 1984.

Evidence of Argentina's growing role in the cocaine trade came in 1988 when police seized more than 1,200 pounds of the drug packaged for export in a single shipment of crated shrimp. The discovery of clandestine airstrips and several cocaine-processing labs near the Bolivian border to the north supported the notion that the cartel was decentralizing its operations into Argentina to avoid detection in the stepped-up drug enforcement activities in the major producing countries. Like Brazil, Argentina produces some of the agents used to process coca and is thus a logical place to set up processing operations. Officials also note a rising incidence of cocaine use among Argentines as the industry takes hold there.

Chile, which shares a common border with Bolivia and Peru, thus far seems to be relatively free of cocaine production and consumption. Individual Chileans are thought to participate in the trade chiefly as couriers, delivering cocaine to the United States and other markets.

The Colombian cartel appears to prefer dealing with right-wing military governments. Panama is best known as a money-laundering center for the region's drug lords. There is evidence that the country's military government also became involved in trafficking as early as 1968, when it came to power under Gen. Omar Torrijos.[22] But Panama's role as a cocaine processing and transshipment hub became more apparent in 1988 when events in that country showed the cocaine industry's power to resist drug-enforcement efforts. General Noriega ignored calls for his resignation as head of the Panama Defense Forces after he was indicted in the United States. In response, Noriega deposed President Eric Arturo Delvalle in February 1988. After his candidate failed to win the presidential election held in May 1989, Noriega annulled the results. He has remained Panama's military strongman and de facto leader ever since, ignoring both the indictments and the strict economic sanctions the Reagan administration imposed on Panama, which depends heavily on American capital for its economic well-being.

Panama is one of several transit points for cocaine shipments to the United States. As U.S. drug-enforcement efforts have intensified in the Bahamas, the Colombian dealers have spread their shipment operations to other Caribbean nations. "Haiti sniffs of a Panama in the making," commented Sen. John Kerry, D-Mass., after evidence was presented in July 1988 before the Senate narcotics subcommittee. Colombian cartel leaders have bought up businesses in Haiti and bribed members of that impoverished island's military leadership to help turn it into a major transit point for the cocaine trade, the panel was told. Col. Jean-Claude Paul, commander of an army barracks in Haiti, is under indictment by a federal grand jury in Miami for cocaine smuggling. Leslie Manigat, Haiti's former president who was deposed in June 1987 in a military coup, claimed he was overthrown because of his efforts to combat the cocaine trade on the island.

Honduras, another of the region's countries under military control, is conveniently located about halfway between Colombia and the United States and appears to have served as a transit point for Colombian cocaine since the early 1980s. A Honduran diplomat was arrested in Miami in May 1988 for smuggling cocaine into the country. Only a month before, Honduran national Juan Ramon Matta Ballesteros was arrested and taken to the United States for trial on drug charges. Matta, the indictment charges, was responsible for getting Colombian cocaine to smugglers in Mexico.

Although weather conditions preclude coca cultivation in Paraguay, the country plays an important role in the cocaine trade as a transit nation. Before he was overthrown in February 1989 by Gen. Andres Rodriguez, Paraguay's military strongman, Alfredo Stroessner, had been accused by the Reagan administration of involvement in cocaine trafficking. Although the government denied the charge, U.S. officials insisted that senior Paraguayan officials were profiting from drug shipments through the country from Bolivia to final export sites in neighboring Brazil.

One of the few important transit points for Colombian cocaine on its way to the United States that boasts strong democratic traditions is Costa Rica. The Central American country lacks the kind of strong military apparatus that has proved amenable to corruption by cocaine traffickers in other transit nations of the region. But its numerous rural airstrips and proximity to the U.S. market make Costa Rica an attractive stopover for the drug trade.

The lure of fabulous profits to be gained from the cocaine trade crosses ideological as well as national boundaries. Several of the region's anticapitalist states, including Cuba and Nicaragua, have been implicated in the region's burgeoning drug business. Cuba, strategically situated near the Florida cocaine market, has long acted as a transshipment point for Colombian cocaine. After repeatedly denying his country's role in the drug trade, Cuban president Fidel Castro finally conceded in July 1989 that fourteen high-ranking officers of the Cuban military had run a cocaine-smuggling operation through Cuba. The ensuing trial ended with the execution of a close associate of Castro's and three other officers.

The government of Nicaragua also has been implicated in cocaine trafficking. Barry Seal, a convicted drug trafficker turned government informant, claimed that in 1984 members of the leftist Sandinista government cooperated with the Colombian cartel in smuggling cocaine into the United States. Seal was later murdered. At the same time, the *contra* rebels who since 1981 have been trying to bring down the Sandinista government with U.S. help have also been charged with engaging in the cocaine trade. The charges, which were the subject of hearings before Senator Kerry's panel in 1988, revolved around alleged participation by *contras* based in neighboring Honduras in a cocaine-trafficking ring run by the Honduran military. Witnesses testified that *contra* groups provided fuel and other services to cocaine couriers in exchange for money they used to conduct their war against the Nicaraguan government.

Recent Developments in the Colombian Cartel

There are signs that the Colombian cocaine cartel is weakening.[23] Competition for North American distribution networks appears to have divided the Medellin and Cali organizations and prompted a wave of assassinations that has left at least eighty people dead in Colombia and dozens more in the United States. Press reports suggest that the feud, which broke out in November 1987, may be causing the cartel greater disruption than any drug-enforcement efforts of recent years.

The conflict emphasizes differences in the two groups' style of business. The Medellin families, under the leadership of Pablo Escobar, are thought to have orchestrated the assassinations of public officials in Colombia, enlisting the support of guerrilla groups such as M-19. According to their logic, the best way to ensure profitability is by intimidating the government through acts of violence to stay out of the way of the trafficking business. The cartel's smaller branch, based in Cali under the joint leadership of Gilberto Rodriguez and Jose Santacruz, appears to favor a less violent approach. By investing their cocaine profits heavily in legitimate enterprises, the Cali branch has sought mainly to incorporate the cocaine industry into Colombia's legal economy.

Notes

1. Merrill Collett, "The Myth of the 'Narcoguerrillas,'" *Nation*, August 13-20, 1988, 134.
2. U.S. Department of State, Bureau of International Narcotics Matters, *International Narcotics Control Strategy Report*, March 1989, 88. See also André McNicoll, *Drug Trafficking: A North-South Perspective* (Ottawa: North-South Institute, 1983), 42-43.
3. Nicholas C. McBride, "U.S. Chemicals Used to Process Illicit Drugs," *Christian Science Monitor*, July 27, 1988, 3.
4. For more information on Peru's guerrilla movement, see Raymond Bonner,

"Peru's War," *New Yorker*, January 4, 1988, 31-58.

5. Alan Riding, "Peru Offers Laws to Combat Terror," *New York Times*, August 21, 1988, 9.
6. Peter Kerr, "Bolivia, with U.S. Aid, Battles Cocaine at the Root," *New York Times*, April 17, 1988, 6.
7. See Clara Germani, "Drug Lords and Public on Collision Path in Bolivia," *Christian Science Monitor*, August 10, 1988, 1; "Now Let's Slay the Other Dragon," *Economist*, July 30-August 5, 1988, 42-43; and "Bolivia: Laid-off Miners Survive by Growing Coca," *Latinamerica Press*, March 17, 1988, 1.
8. Rensselaer W. Lee III, "Dimensions of the South American Cocaine Industry" (Paper presented at the Latin American Narcotics Trade and United States Security conference, Mississippi State University, June 16-17, 1988).
9. Buenaventura Marcelo, a professor at Peru's National Agrarian University, published a report on water pollution by the coca industry in September 1987. See James F. Smith, "Aerial Attacks on Coca? Peru Stalls U.S. Plan," *Los Angeles Times*, June 30, 1988, I12.
10. George Shultz spoke August 8, 1988, before a group of Bolivians and members of the press in La Paz, Bolivia.
11. Bruce M. Bagley, "Colombia and the War on Drugs," *Foreign Affairs* (Fall 1988): 74-75.
12. Collett, "Myth of the Narcoguerrillas," 113.
13. FARC helped the peasants fix minimum prices for the leaves they sold to the cartel. See Fabio Castillo, *Los jinetes de la cocaina* (Bogota: Editorial Documentos Periodisticos, 1987).
14. Bagley, "Colombia and the War on Drugs," 84.
15. Collett, "Myth of the Narcoguerrillas," 134.
16. The narcotics subcommittee, chaired by Sen. John Kerry, D-Mass., held hearings on the international drug trade July 11, 12, and 14, 1988.
17. Bagley, "Colombia and the War on Drugs," 77.
18. Ibid., 82.
19. See James Chace, "Getting to Sack the General," *New York Review of Books*, April 28, 1988, 49-55.
20. Alan Riding, "Brazil Now a Vital Crossroad for Latin Cocaine Traffickers," *New York Times*, August 28, 1988, 1.
21. Mac Margolis, "Rio Drug Lords Reign with Fear and Favor," *Washington Post*, August 13, 1988, A15.
22. See Larry Rohter, "America's Blind Eye," *New York Times Magazine*, May 29, 1988, 24.
23. Alan Riding, "Gangs in Colombia Feud over Cocaine," *New York Times*, August 23, 1988, 1.

2 Channels of Cocaine Distribution

Because the biggest markups in cocaine prices occur in the U.S. market, Rensselaer Lee of Global Advisory Services believes the Colombian cartels may be involved in at least the first stage of the U.S. distribution network. "I'm pretty sure the Colombians are involved in wholesaling," he says. "They would not simply drop the cocaine at the U.S. border." Cocaine prices skyrocket upon the drug's arrival in the United States. Lee describes a typical progression that begins with a border price, paid by the first buyer of the smuggled product. Large dealers then pay a wholesale price for these 100-200 kilo bundles, which they reduce in size and purity and sell for a distribution price, paid by rings that dominate regional markets. These in turn sell still smaller and less concentrated quantities to local dealers, who then sell it to users for a final, retail price. Lee speculates that the Colombians control the trade through at least one or two links of the U.S. distribution chain. The presence of Colombian nationals, who constitute the largest South American population in the United States, facilitates the cartels' control over the cocaine market here, Lee added.

After transporting cocaine over the border, Lee says, the cartels sell the product to their own distributors, who then resell it to dealers to get double the wholesale price. The National Narcotics Intelligence Consumers Committee (NNICC), formed in 1978 to coordinate information on illegal drugs gathered by all the federal agencies involved in drug-enforcement activities, agrees with this analysis. "Colombian nationals continued to be the principal producers and distributors of cocaine hydrochloride sold in the United States," the agency stated in its annual report.[1]

The cartels' efficiency at processing and shipping is equally evident at the secondary distribution level in the United States, where their involvement dates from the late 1970s. For several years, South Florida was besieged by violent killings that claimed more than 100 deaths in 1981 alone. In the wake of the "cocaine wars," the Colombians wrested control of the cocaine wholesale market from the Cuban Americans who until then had dominated the Miami-based trade.

Cocaine powder appears to be readily available in large, multi-kilo quantities in all large U.S. cities, the government reports. So efficient is the import apparatus that there is a glut in the U.S. cocaine market despite the growing demand for crack. Peter Reuter of the Rand Corporation estimates that cocaine passes through about six transactions between its importation in 200-kilo bundles and the retail level. The numerous transactions help shield any one dealer from contact with too many customers and potential informants. At each transaction level, the drug increases in price. According to NNICC estimates, by the end of 1988 cocaine sold for $11,000-$34,000 a kilo at the wholesale level, the first transaction within the United States. This was the lowest wholesale price range ever recorded, continuing a trend the NNICC attributes to the drug's widespread availability (Figure 2-1). As recently as 1984, cocaine powder sold for $40,000-$50,000 a kilo wholesale, and the price has dropped steadily ever since.

The street price for one gram of cocaine has been less sensitive, although it has dropped somewhat since 1984, when it stood at $100-$120 per gram. By the end of 1987, a gram of cocaine was going for $80-$100 in most areas. The markup from cocaine's point of entry into the United States to the street, then, was still about 200-400 percent, even at those depressed prices.

The robust markup of cocaine prices is even more remarkable in light of the drug's progressive dilution as it passes through the distribution chain. DEA can determine this change by analyzing the purity of the substance seized in large and small packages. Cocaine sold by the kilo, the standard wholesale quantity, averaged high purity levels of 85-90 percent in 1987. Average one-ounce quantities, cut with inert substances for sale to street retailers, were 75-80 percent pure. One-gram single doses, a common size for final street sales to users, averaged just over 50 percent pure, about half the purity level of cocaine hydrochloride as it leaves the processing laboratories, but more than twice the purity level commonly sold to users as recently as 1981. The fact that users are paying less for higher concentrations of cocaine is further evidence that the glut continues in the U.S. market (Table 2-1).

Cocaine smugglers' favorite mode of shipping remains the general aviation aircraft. Ever since Carlos Lehder and other managers of the cartels' downstream activities set up fueling and transshipment points throughout the Caribbean and Central America, small private planes have been the preferred vehicle for delivering cocaine to its first destination in the United States. But other shipment modes are also becoming more popular. From 1986 to 1987 the portion of cocaine seized from private planes fell from nearly half to just over a third of all seizures at the point of entry in the United States, the government reports. Almost half the cocaine imports arrived aboard seagoing vessels, almost equally divided between commercial and private ships.

Figure 2-1 *Trends in Cocaine Availability, Perceived Risk of Trying, and Use in Past Year by High School Seniors, 1975-1988*

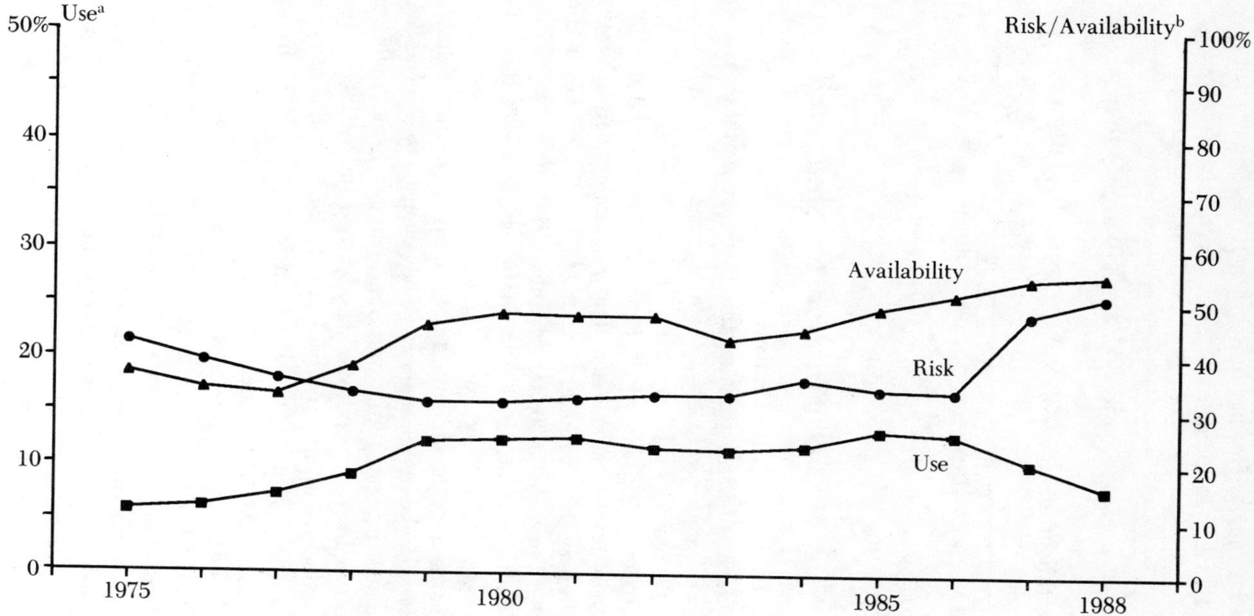

[a] Use: Percentage using once or more in past twelve months.
[b] Risk: Percentage saying great risk of harm in using once or twice. Availability: Percentage saying fairly easy or very easy to get.

Source: L. D. Johnston, P. M. O'Malley, and J. G. Bachman, *Drug Use, Drinking, and Smoking: National Survey Results from High School, College, and Young Adult Populations*, U.S. Department of Health and Human Services, National Institute on Drug Abuse, 1989.

Table 2-1 Cocaine Trafficking Indicators, 1985-1988

	1985	1986	1987	1988
Retail Purity	50-60%	55-65%	50+%	70%
Prices[a]				
Wholesale (kilogram)	$30-$50	$22-$45	$12-$40	$11-$34
Retail (gram)	$100	$80-$120	$80-$120	$50-$120

[a]End-of-year prices; wholesale prices in thousands of dollars.
Source: National Narcotics Intelligence Consumers Committee (NNICC), *The NNICC Report 1988: The Supply of Illicit Drugs to the United States,* April 1989.

Miami—First U.S. Destination for Smuggled Cocaine

Although the cocaine distribution network has dispersed with the spread of crack's popularity, Miami remains the Medellin cartel's main base of operations in this country. One way of measuring a city's role in the drug trade is by its record of felony cases: From 1984 until mid-1988, the Southern District of Florida, which includes Miami—a city of 450,000—had more than 1,350 felony cases. This was more than any other U.S. district, including the Southern District of New York, which comprises New York City and its 7,000,000 inhabitants.[2]

The "cigarette boat," a small, fast speedboat, is one of the smugglers' preferred means of getting past coast guard surveillance in southern Florida, the main point of entry for Colombian cocaine. Most cocaine arrives in Florida aboard small aircraft, however. Gary Wayne Betzner, a convicted drug-smuggler-turned-informant, told a Senate subcommittee how it works. A former cropduster who learned the art of evading radar detection while in antisubmarine warfare training in the navy, Betzner testified that he regularly lost DEA chase planes while transporting cocaine into Florida. "All you needed to do was to be able to fly below the horizon, below the radar, and come up in the blind spots between the radars," he said.[3] The cartels pay handsomely for such expertise. Before he was convicted in 1986, Betzner received $40,000 per flight from George Morales, a Colombian national based in Miami who also is serving a sentence in a U.S. prison for drug smuggling.

The Colombian drug lords have facilitated the shipment of their goods by bribing government officials, judges, and police all along the cocaine route to the United States. And this activity does not stop at the border. The fabulous profits to be made from the drug trade have proved too great a temptation for some police officers in Miami. In the most widely publicized scandal, known as the "River Cop" case, sixteen officers of the

1,000-member Miami police force were convicted in 1985 of participating in a local drug-smuggling ring. The officers were charged with raiding a cocaine-smuggler's boat on the Miami River and stealing the 900-pound cargo. The River Cop case prompted federal agencies to investigate an additional 150 of the city's police officers.

After 1981, when drug-enforcement agencies intensified their interdiction efforts in and around southern Florida, cocaine runners began bypassing the area and landing their aircraft and vessels in neighboring jurisdictions. Drug pilots departing from Haiti, the Bahamas, and other nearby transit points are able to fly farther north or west to land on makeshift runways in pastures or country roads in rural Georgia, Louisiana, Alabama, Mississippi, and Texas. The move has been accompanied by a wave of corruption charges against local sheriffs and other law-enforcement officers in these states. The $50,000-$100,000 paid to bribe a sheriff to look the other way for a single shipment of cocaine far exceeds what a rural law-enforcement officer earns in a year.[4] For the cartels, it is an almost negligible business expense. Rural drops also pose few risks of detection, once a safe landing site is found. A drug runner can offload his cargo and take off again in a matter of minutes, while his accomplices drive the shipment to Miami by car.

Miami is not only the main import center for cocaine but also the busiest U.S. city on the money-laundering side of the trade, being conveniently located within minutes by air of "safe havens" like the Bahamas, where strict bank-secrecy laws make it all but impossible for U.S. drug-enforcement authorities to uncover the trail of profits from drug sales. Miami serves as the final collection center for cocaine profits made all over the country.

The region is made even more attractive by its unusual banking regulatory system. Florida law places bank regulation exclusively in the hands of elected officials, a practice that critics say invites corruption.[5] They cite such examples as Sunshine State Bank, a Miami financial institution owned by a family of Cuban immigrants that was used for laundering drug money before it was closed in 1986.

Although the full scope of south Florida's money-laundering operations is unknown, the drug trade is thought to bring in about as much money annually as tourism ($20 billion) and agriculture ($16 billion), the state's leading legitimate industries. In 1986 state authorities seized more than $1 billion in illegal drugs, an amount thought to be only a small portion of the total volume of cocaine and other drugs that pass through south Florida.[6] Once it has been laundered, either locally or in foreign bank accounts, a good part of the Miami-based dealers' profits return to the local economy, where they are invested in legitimate businesses and used to purchase cars, jewelry, and other expensive consumer goods that have come to be the hallmark of higher-level drug dealers.

New York City—A Growing Base of Operation

Drug interdiction efforts in recent years have forced the cartels to diversify their initial destination points, with New York City and states along the U.S.-Mexican border serving as important entry ways for cocaine. Also in reaction to stepped-up drug-enforcement efforts, the cartels have largely moved their limited cocaine-processing operations from the United States back to South America. The number of cocaine-conversion laboratories discovered in New York and Florida, the main centers for this activity, has fallen significantly since 1985.

New York City is the cocaine industry's second most important base of operations on the East Coast. There too, the cocaine trade is tightly controlled by the Colombians. When they first penetrated the United States in the early 1980s, the Medellin and Cali organizations carved up the North American market, each controlling distinct areas of the country. The Medellin contingent claimed rights to drug profits in Miami, Los Angeles, and Western Europe, while the smaller and less violent Cali group enjoyed more or less exclusive rights to other cities in California and Texas, as well as New York City and the increasingly lucrative markets of Stamford, Connecticut, and other outlying suburban cities. Growing crack use in these smaller cities has transformed the regional cocaine business into an industry worth hundreds of millions of dollars each year.

Most cocaine destined for New York is flown in directly from Colombia by private plane or driven by couriers from Florida. The Cali organization in New York then sells the drug to some forty or fifty local high-level distributors. These in turn sell smaller quantities to thousands of lower-level dealers throughout the area. The dealers either sell the drug as cocaine hydrochloride or "cook" the powder and sell it as crack. By this point, the drug has passed from the Colombian organization into the hands of traditional local crime organizations. In one case, twenty alleged leaders of the Lucchese crime family, one of the five biggest local Mafia organizations, were charged with distributing and selling cocaine. Although the trial ended August 26, 1988, in acquittal for all the defendants, it produced ample evidence of Mafia involvement in the cocaine distribution business.

But the steady rise in violent crimes in the New York metropolitan area since 1985 also suggests that the Mafia shares its role in distributing and selling cocaine with other groups that have risen to power with the crack boom. Mafia organizations traditionally have directed their acts of violence against rivals, but less often involved family members of targeted victims, and rarely innocent bystanders. Today, New York City police report that a higher percentage, more than a third, of the city's homicides involve drugs than before. They attribute the increase to the growing use of crack and the more ruthless practices of the groups that sell it, including gangs of Jamaican, Dominican, and Cuban youths.

The new generation of crime organizations are less tightly structured than the traditional Mafia families. As a result, they have less clear-cut boundaries and often fight with each other over territory. Their turf wars have turned entire neighborhoods into battlefields. New York's crack traders spend much of their earnings to arm themselves, sending couriers as far as Texas, Alabama, and Georgia to buy more powerful guns than they can obtain in New York. The Uzis and other semiautomatic weapons they can buy legally in other states are then easily converted into fully automatic machine guns capable of discharging bursts of twenty bullets or more in seconds.

The geographic distribution of New York City's cocaine trade can be pieced together from the crime statistics. The violence accompanying the cocaine trade is concentrated in upper Manhattan, Queens, and Brooklyn. While the citywide homicide rate rose by 6 percent in 1987 over the year before, the number of killings in Queens, a predominantly residential area, rose by 25 percent for the second year in a row. In one incident in May 1988, the Queens home of an imprisoned drug dealer, Lorenzo Nichols, was firebombed. Nichols's disabled sister was killed in the blaze, her young son severely burned. Three months earlier, a young police officer, Edward Byrne, was gunned down in Queens as he stood guard outside the home of a witness in a drug case. The shooting, which shocked the New York community, was further evidence of the shift in control over the lower levels of cocaine distribution from the Mafia to the gangs. Unlike more established crime organizations in the city, this new generation of drug dealers does not hesitate to kill law-enforcement agents who interfere with business.

In upper Manhattan, the Do-Wops, the John Johns, and the P.C. Boys are among a dozen or more gangs that control the retail crack trade. Each group claims monopoly interest on its turf, which can be one or more square city blocks or long corridors that follow both sides of a street for several blocks. In some neighborhoods, groups of Dominican gangs appear to share larger territories.[7] Challenges over territorial rights are met with gunfire, often street assassinations in broad daylight, in an apparent bid to frighten rivals or informants. As many as 500 homicides were attributed to these gangs from 1983 to 1985.

The fall in drug profits brought on by the recent cocaine glut has intensified the two Colombian groups' rivalry over the lucrative New York market. As oversupply forced down cocaine prices, the larger and more violent Medellin group began targeting the New York market for takeover beginning in 1986. While prices have fallen in most cities, some, like New York, have experienced a dramatic increase in demand for crack, which has slowed the price fall and widened the price differentials among cities. In 1988, as prices fell to around $10,000 a kilo in the Medellin-controlled Miami market, they held steady at around $18,000 in the New York area. It was then that the Medellin forces launched their offensive to wrest New York from their competitors in the Cali group. More than a dozen Colombians were murdered in New York City in what authorities there predicted was only the first stage of a prolonged struggle for control over the New York market. This time, the Cali organization seemed prepared to fight the competition on its own terms, hiring "enforcers," or paid assassins, to defend their turf.[8] Both sides also began informing police on one another, leading to numerous cocaine seizures and arrests in both New York and Florida. Evidence that the cartels were using informants to conduct their conflict came in August 1988, when police arrested Hernando Grajales Rizo, the acknowledged head of the Cali group's New York operations, and seized two tons of pure cocaine at his residence in Queens. The seizure, the largest ever in New York City, came after police received an anonymous tip, thought to have come from the Medellin group.[9]

The question remains why cocaine prices are falling at a time when demand for cocaine products is growing and their supply presumably is being hampered by stepped-up law-enforcement efforts in the fields, at the border, and in the streets. The August 1988 New York City bust removed more than 30 million vials of crack from the streets, but not even the turf war and police seizures appear to have affected cocaine prices or availability. The initial wholesale price fell from a maximum of $55,000 per kilo in 1983 to as little as $12,000 in 1988. According to the market-oriented explanation, the increased South American production of coca leaf in the 1980s has far outweighed the rise in demand for crack, while demand for cocaine powder has remained fairly stable. As a result, dealers have to sell greater quantities of the drug to realize the same profits, but they are stymied in their efforts to expand their clientele of cocaine users in established markets (Figure 2-2).

Reuter offers another interesting, albeit hypothetical, explanation of falling cocaine prices that reflects the peculiar economic forces at work in the illicit drug market. "If you accept that this is a competitive market, as more dealers get experienced, the price will tend to go down because each of them finds ways to evade seizures of drug shipments and arrest and therefore to lower his distribution costs." Even with intensified interdiction, it will be the novices who are most frequently caught. "So even if they are seizing more cocaine, the number of experienced dealers keeps going up to meet the expanding demand." As a result, supplies continue to grow, even exceeding demand, pushing prices down.

One group of distributors that would seem to support Reuter's hypothesis are the Jamaican crack dealers. Although Colombian nationals

Figure 2-2 Trends in Cocaine Use during Previous Month by Age Group, 1974-1988

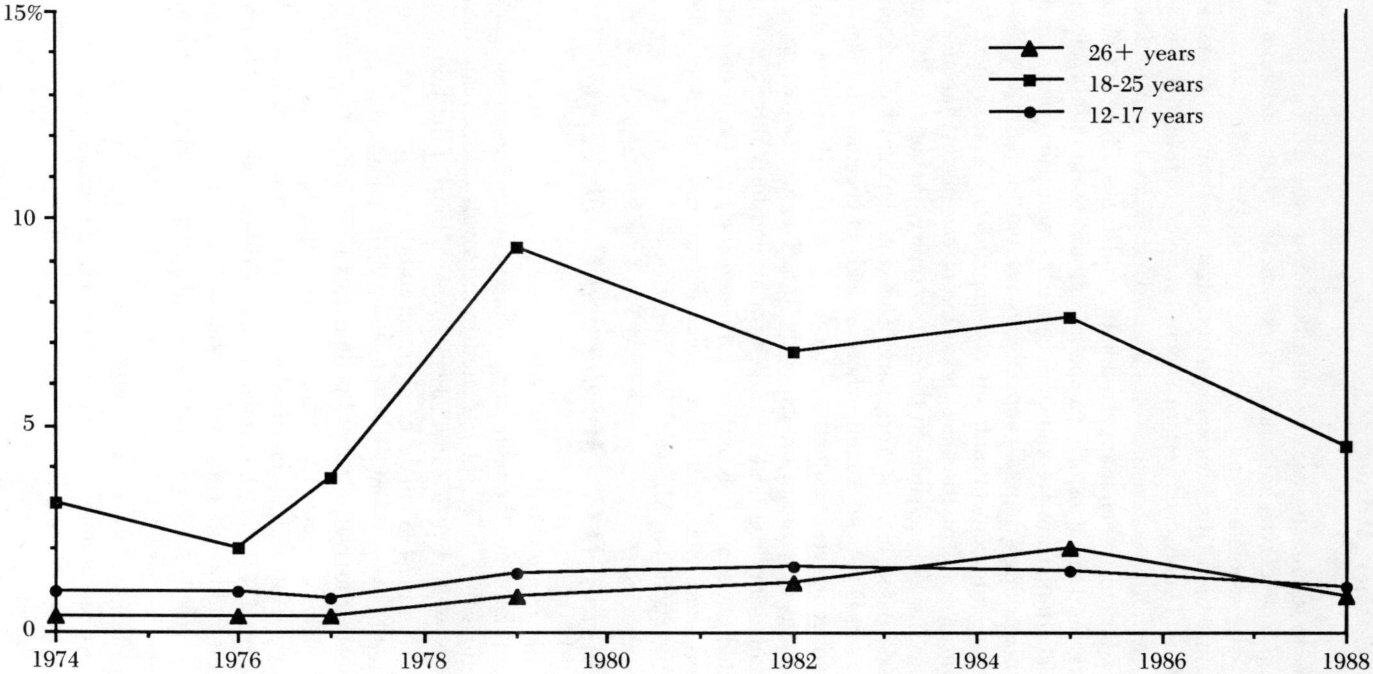

Note: In 1974, 1976, and 1977 the estimates were less than .5% for the 26+ years age group.

Source: U.S. Department of Health and Human Services, National Institute on Drug Abuse, National Household Survey on Drug Abuse.

continue to dominate cocaine distribution in the United States, the Jamaicans have carved out a large market niche in the distribution phases between the wholesale and final retail levels. Active in the marijuana market since the 1970s, they work in organizations known as posses, a term inspired by Hollywood western movies popular in Kingston and other poverty-ridden towns on the Caribbean island. They began to take over the crack business when it appeared in the mid-1980s. Like the Colombian exporters, the Jamaicans bring a special cultural tradition to their chosen trade. "The Jamaicans are known to be a very industrious, very organized and hard-working group of people," says Sgt. Pat Moyer of the U.S. Park Police drug-enforcement unit in Washington, D.C., an expert on the Jamaican drug distribution network. One of the biggest Jamaican organizations, The Untouchables, is thought to typify the business structure of the posses. Based in New York City, The Untouchables has branches in Washington, D.C., and Miami, where it deals in cocaine, illegal weapons sales, and contract assassination. According to the Bureau of Alcohol, Tobacco, and Firearms, a branch of the U.S. Treasury Department, some 10,000 Jamaican drug dealers worked for around forty different gangs in the United States in 1988. As they saturated the East Coast markets, the Jamaicans were thought to have spread out to penetrate other potential crack markets in the Midwest and West.

Washington, D.C.—Murder and Crack Capital

The Jamaicans are also unusually violent, even by the standards of the new gangs that dominate the retail drug business. In cities like New York and Washington, they have not hesitated to kill rivals to dominate the local markets. New York police attribute more than a third of the 1,691 murders in the city during 1987 to the crack trade, and they say many of those were committed by posse members. A trademark of Jamaican crack dealers and a sign of their arrival in a metropolitan area is execution-style murder. A spate of such killings in 1987 and 1988, including the daring murder of a man stopped at a light in rush-hour traffic, signaled to authorities in Washington, D.C., that the Jamaicans had arrived. Unlike La Cosa Nostra and other traditional crime organizations, which "tend to settle accounts among themselves," Moyer says, "the Jamaicans are trying to intimidate everyone. They seem to have a lower regard for the sanctity of human life." In 1988, the District of Columbia registered a record 372 killings, the highest per capita murder rate in the nation. The number of assaults with guns rose by more than half over the period, a trend the police attributed to drug dealers.

The posses have not widened their market share by violence alone. "All drugs coming from Jamaica are considered to be of better quality," Moyer says. They also provide crack buyers a kind of discount known as a "working 50," a rock that is slightly bigger than the standard $50 size. That way, a buyer can smoke some and resell the rest for $50, "so you can get your money's worth and still get high." The end result of the violence, the quality of the product, and the ingenuity is that Jamaicans have achieved greater control over the packaging, marketing, and sales end of the cocaine industry than most drug dealers in the U.S. market. "They get it, cut it, and run it, controlling the distribution all the way down to the street level," says Moyer.

There is another factor that favors well-organized distributors and dealers like the Jamaicans: The illicit nature of the drug business hampers efficient nationwide distribution of drugs. As a result, there are marked price differences among cities. When the price of crack plunged in New York in 1987, for example, the posses moved into Washington, D.C., where they could get a better price. Since then, crack has become the most popular drug in the nation's capital. Moyer says the standard price of crack in Washington is still double or triple the New York price, and in some instances "dealers can sell a $5 chunk of crack they got in New York for $30 here."

Just why crack prices differ so greatly is unclear. "It is clearly not related to demographics," comments Reuter. He cites the examples of Los Angeles and Miami, both of which have large populations of heavy cocaine users. Prices, however, are low in both cities, apparently insensitive to the high demand. In Miami, for example, a kilo of cocaine that as recently as 1982 cost $50,000 could be bought for $10,000 in 1988. The average price for a kilo of cocaine in Los Angeles fell from $40,000 in 1984 to $13,000 in mid-1988. Reuter speculates that because both cities are heavily used as transit points for cocaine imports, the distribution costs at the street level are lower, making the final product cheaper there than in other cities.

Judging from their activities selling crack in Washington, D.C., since their arrival in 1985, the Jamaicans have refined drug distribution patterns. Like traditional crime organizations, they group themselves in separate "cells" to insulate dealers from one another to prevent a single confession from incriminating an entire organization. But the Jamaicans have introduced an even more elaborate system of stash houses, gate houses, and other checkpoints to prevent police infiltration.

Ever since the Colombians introduced the idea in the early 1980s, electronic paging devices, or beepers, have been standard equipment for drug dealers. In a typical transaction, one person with a drug shipment to deliver will dial a telephone number assigned to the dealer's beeper and leave a message, which is then relayed automatically to the beeper. More recent models are equipped with display screens that can receive any number of number-coded messages. The object of this elaborate communications network is to elude detection by police and to limit the number of face-to-face contacts among individuals—and potential informants—along the distribution chain.

But the Jamaicans are credited with taking this cat-and-mouse game a step further. Because regular telephones can easily be tapped by the police, posse members often use cellular telephones, exchanging information on dropoff points and new deals while driving around the city to elude detection. They often work out of apartments in the same poor urban neighborhoods where crack is in heavy demand, paying the occupants' rent in exchange for the right to use the place to complete their transactions. Like other middlemen, most Jamaicans hire local youths to sell their product on the streets. As one drug-enforcement official said, "Selling drugs gives status to young people. With the money they earn, they can buy fine clothes, cars, and jewelry." Many street-level crack dealers are as young as twelve or thirteen. For these young entrepreneurs, the trade is hard to resist. "A drug dealer can make $1,000 in a week selling crack just for being on the payroll, no matter how much he sells," Moyer says. "Compare that to working for the minimum wage at McDonalds, where he'd clear maybe $70 a week." At the bottom of the distribution ladder are even younger children, who make as much as $15 a day collecting and turning in empty crack vials for recycling.

The efficiency of the posses is unrivaled: "D.C. has more drugs per square foot than anywhere in the nation," Moyer says. In addition to the Jamaicans' salesmanship, he attributes the rapid spread of drug use there to the area's relatively high per capita income and the mobility of its population, which varies from a daytime high of 1.2 million to only 630,000 at night, as government employees and other workers in the city leave for the suburbs. This high mobility may also explain why the Washington suburbs in Northern Virginia and Maryland were found by a 1988 Rand Corporation study to have the heaviest drug use of any suburban area in the country.[10]

Located between Miami and New York City, Washington receives its cocaine and crack shipments from both cities. The crack traffic from New York grew heavier in 1987, as dealers tried capitalize on the higher prices they could charge in the expanding Washington crack market. Initially, most crack appears to have arrived by car, as dealers could drive their cargo from New York in only a few hours. After police stepped up their surveillance along the north-south interstate system, which became known as "Cocaine Alley," the dealers turned to the frequent air shuttle, passenger train, and bus services that link the two cities. They can easily take cocaine to Washington, sell it, and return to New York in a day. Later, as local police forces began making successful drug busts at Union Station and National Airport, the New York dealers increasingly sent underage couriers to ship and sell their product in the Washington market. If caught, youths under eighteen are prosecuted as minors and, if found guilty, receive lighter sentences than in New York, where the cutoff age is sixteen.

Illegal substances can be bought at any time of day in Washington's numerous open-air drug markets. In some areas of the city, dealers openly hawk their wares, making hand signals to passing motorists to indicate what they are selling and for what price.

Los Angeles—Gang Headquarters

Los Angeles has been the center of the West Coast crack trade ever since the drug arrived between 1984 and 1985. Some 500 street gangs made up of black, Asian, and Hispanic youths are widely believed to control distribution in the black neighborhoods of south Los Angeles. The Crips and the Bloods, the city's two dominant street gangs with an estimated 60,000 members between them, were featured on the cover of *Newsweek* in 1988, as they became equated with the spreading crack trade. The gangs, an outgrowth of the racial turmoil that erupted in the Watts riots of 1965, have been in existence for a number of years.[11] Their areas of control in the poor black and Hispanic neighborhoods of south and central Los Angeles are better defined than those of the newer groups that dominate the East Coast market. But turf wars are a common ingredient in the crack trade here as well. More than 2,400 people have lost their lives in drug-related violence in Los Angeles during the 1980s, almost 400 in 1987 alone. Many killings occur in daylight by gun-wielding youths who spray their victims with machine-gun fire from passing cars. Often Crips kill Bloods over market share. But the gangs are so loosely organized that affiliation with one group does not necessarily preclude competition, and different "sets" of youths belonging to the same gang often fight for turf.

In their attempt to disrupt the local cocaine trade, California police have focused on the street gangs. In September 1988 California attorney general John K. Van de Kamp called "the transformation of Los Angeles street gangs into full-fledged organized crime networks that deal in violence, death, and cocaine" the state's most worrisome crime problem.[12] Although he described the gangs as less tightly structured than traditional crime syndicates, Van de Kamp identified them as the main distributing agents working for the top Colombian cocaine importers. The Medellin contingent controls California's cocaine market. The attorney general also released a report entitled "Organized Crime in California 1987," in which it was estimated that 150 members of the Medellin group control about six distinct regional cocaine distribution and money-laundering rings from their headquarters in California. The official called the nearly 400 murders in 1987 "grim reminders that groups like the Crips and the Bloods are no longer street gangs in the traditional sense of the term. They are far-flung distribution networks for Colombian cocaine—with elaborate organizations and murderous profit motive for eliminating the competition."

But another study, conducted by sociology professors at the University of Southern California, disputes the notion that the street gangs are primarily responsible for crack's distribution on the West Coast. After examining police records of local cocaine-related arrests, Malcolm W. Klein and Cheryl L. Maxson found that only a quarter of the cases involved gang members. They concluded that the Los Angeles cocaine trade remains predominantly in the hands of the city's traditional drug dealers, which include West Coast branches of the Mafia as well as other highly cohesive ethnic crime syndicates made up of Cuban, Israeli, Hungarian, and Russian immigrants.[13]

Whatever their role at home, law-enforcement authorities all over the country agree that the Los Angeles gangs have played a major part in spreading the crack trade to other cities. Oversupply has pushed down cocaine prices in Los Angeles as it has along the East Coast cocaine corridor. Wholesale prices in Los Angeles fell from an average $40,000 in 1984 to $13,000 by early 1988. In their search for higher profits, the gangs have set up franchise operations in thirty localities in California and many other cities along the West Coast, including Portland, Seattle, and Tacoma and as far north as Anchorage. More recently, beginning in early 1987, the Los Angeles gangs also began migrating eastward to dozens of cities in the West and the Midwest, where they frequently bring in profits two to three times higher than they can make at home. In the past few years, members of the Bloods and the Crips have been arrested for crack peddling in many cities that had previously been free of the drug, including Las Vegas, Phoenix, Denver, and St. Louis. The FBI estimates the Los Angeles gangs operate in more than forty cities across the country.

In some cities where the Bloods and Crips have been observed, the Los Angeles distributors initially meet little or no resistance from local youths who might be expected to challenge them for control of the lucrative trade. Omaha, Nebraska, for example, had no gangs before the Californians moved in. In other cities, such as Denver, indigenous gangs have proved no match for the Bloods and the Crips, which have used violence and marketing know-how to sweep such "wanna-bes" out of the picture. In other cities, the Los Angeles gangs have moved in to occupy a vacuum created when local authorities destroy an existing distribution ring. In Kansas City, for example, the gangs moved in shortly after the authorities dispersed a Miami-based Jamaican posse that had introduced crack to the community in 1985. More than 200 posse members were convicted, and the rest left the city. But the Los Angeles gangs soon stepped in to take their place. Like their colleagues in the upper echelons of the cocaine business, the Bloods and the Crips have ambiguous business relations, cooperating in certain areas of the trade while killing one another off in others. The Los Angeles gangs have been known to collaborate in setting up business in a new city, only to resume competition once the crack market has become established. As the market matures, the gangs may face further competition from local youths who have learned the trade while selling crack on the street for the Los Angeles gangs.

The market potential for the crack trade remains strong in some large communities such as Chicago and St. Louis where the drug has not yet taken hold.

Crack: The Drug of the '80s

The source of a growing portion of cocaine profits along the entire cocaine distribution chain is crack. Named for the crackling sound it makes when smoked, crack is made by mixing cocaine powder with baking soda, which acts as a catalyst, and water. The mixture is boiled to remove the kerosene and other impurities used in breaking down the coca leaves to paste. "All it takes is twenty minutes in the microwave," says Sgt. Moyer.

Crack is sold in small rocks resembling cream-colored gravel for as little as $10 each and is smoked in a pipe over a continuous heat source, such as a butane lighter. "Crack users say it is the best rush they've ever had, better than sex," Moyer says. Unlike cocaine powder, crack is considered to be highly addictive. Cocaine powder, a popular remedy for hay fever in the nineteenth century, constricts the vessels in the nose, limiting the additional pleasure that can be had by increasing the amount of powder snorted at a single session. No such threshold effect occurs with smoking crack, which causes a brief rush within just eight to ten seconds of inhaling the drug. Because the effect wears off within minutes, users are likely to consume much larger quantities of crack than cocaine powder.

Crack has not penetrated the United States as thoroughly as cocaine powder. The crack market is mostly confined to large metropolitan areas, but in a few cities it is readily available, selling for $10-$30 a quarter-gram rock. Even at these low prices, selling crack is highly profitable. In Washington, D.C., Moyer says, cocaine powder can be bought for $1,500 per ounce (28 grams). Once cooked, the mixture yields about 25 grams—100 quarter-gram rocks of crack. These sell for $25 each, so, says Moyer, "you take in $2,500 for your original expenditure of $1,500." With such a big markup, selling crack is more profitable than selling cocaine powder, despite the low retail price for each dose. Because the "cooking" process is fast and does not require sophisticated equipment, it is often worth the risk of police detection for retailers to transform cocaine hydrochloride into crack before selling the substance on the street. Although some crack has been seized at the wholesale level, in fact, most crack is intercepted at the point of sale on the street.

The market for crack has remained largely stable since 1986, but its distribution is becoming more centralized. In late 1985 and early 1986, shortly after crack first appeared in the United States, distribution was limited to certain neighborhoods, where it was sold on the street or in "crack houses," where users could both buy and consume the drug. This is still the most frequent distribution pattern for crack. But since then, a few large wholesale crack-producing and distributing organizations have appeared, controlling the market in one or more cities.

Money-Laundering

The final step in the cocaine-distribution process entails the laundering of the proceeds of the trade and their investment in legitimate businesses, real estate, government securities, and the stock market. Because drugs are sold almost exclusively for cash, mostly in small bills, profits are bulky and hard to conceal or invest inconspicuously. For this reason, an efficient laundering operation is an essential component of the trafficker's business. The large drug rings collect the cash profits from street sales and ship the money to central collection centers. The biggest center for money-laundering is Miami, but drug interdiction efforts there have prompted traffickers to disperse their money-laundering activities. Today, southern Florida and New York City are the main collection centers for the East Coast cocaine trade. West Coast distributors generally pool their earnings in Los Angeles or Houston.

Once collected, there are various ways to launder the profits of illegal drug sales. One is by "smurfing," the purchase of cashier's checks or money orders from many different financial institutions. Careful smurfing allows dealers to get around the Bank Secrecy Act of 1970, which requires banks to report to the Treasury Department all cash transactions of more than $10,000. In 1985, Congress stiffened the criminal charges for violations of the law's reporting requirements. It also passed the Money Laundering Control Act of 1986, which made money-laundering a criminal felony. But as long as couriers purchase checks in amounts under $10,000, they still can avoid detection. The checks and money orders are made out to an individual who receives them through the mail or by personal delivery and deposits them into a bank account. From there, the money can be transferred to other accounts, either in the United States or abroad.

As the volume of drug imports has grown in the 1980s, so too have the profits to be laundered through the U.S. banking system. The sheer amount of drug profits generated in the United States alone—estimated at more than $100 billion a year—has overwhelmed the government's ability to monitor wire transfers, much less detect and prosecute offenders. With so much money at stake, drug exporters are adopting more sophisticated ways to recover their profits.

Until he was arrested in 1989, the Medellin cartel employed an economist and banking specialist, Eduardo Martinez Romero, to oversee its money-laundering operations in the United States. According to an indictment handed down by the Justice Department, Martinez directed a money-laundering operation based in Los Angeles that allegedly processed $1.2 billion in drug profits before it was uncovered by officials in March 1989. Known as "*La Mina*," or "The Mine," the operation allegedly used a jewelry store as its front and deposited drug profits in U.S. banks, including Citibank and the Bank of New York. From there, the funds were transferred by wire to the Medellin cartel's accounts at banks in South America.

Clearly, much of the profit from the drug trade is used by local traffickers for personal consumption. Indeed, many convicted dealers were betrayed by their expensive tastes, which drew the attention of the authorities and led to their arrest. Heavy gold jewelry, expensive clothes, and expensive cars are often the first things retail drug dealers invest in. Moyer described one street dealer who claimed he made $7,800 in a good week and kept his earnings in a shoe box at home. Although he was too young to drive, Moyer said, the dealer had bought a Mercedes-Benz and a Blazer. "He planned to keep selling [drugs] until he had $60,000 in cash and a house." Dealers higher up on the distribution ladder frequently invest in expensive real estate or legitimate businesses.

But the bulk of cocaine profits, those destined for the large organizations that control the market, are shipped out of the country to "safe havens." Occasionally dealers wire their earnings directly to foreign bank accounts, but much of the drug profit is carried physically out of the country. Money pooled in Los Angeles, for example, often is driven to Miami, where it is shipped by commercial or private aircraft to neighboring countries of the Caribbean and Central America. Panama, as pointed out in Chapter 1, is the main Latin American location of money-laundering activities. Bank-secrecy laws in the Cayman Islands make this British dependency in the Caribbean a favorite money-laundering capital. Money-laundering activities are also reported in the Bahamas, the Netherlands Antilles, Antigua, Montserrat, and the Turks and Caicos Islands, all of which offer proximity to the United States and favorable banking regulations.

Figure 2-3 *Drug Distribution Routes*

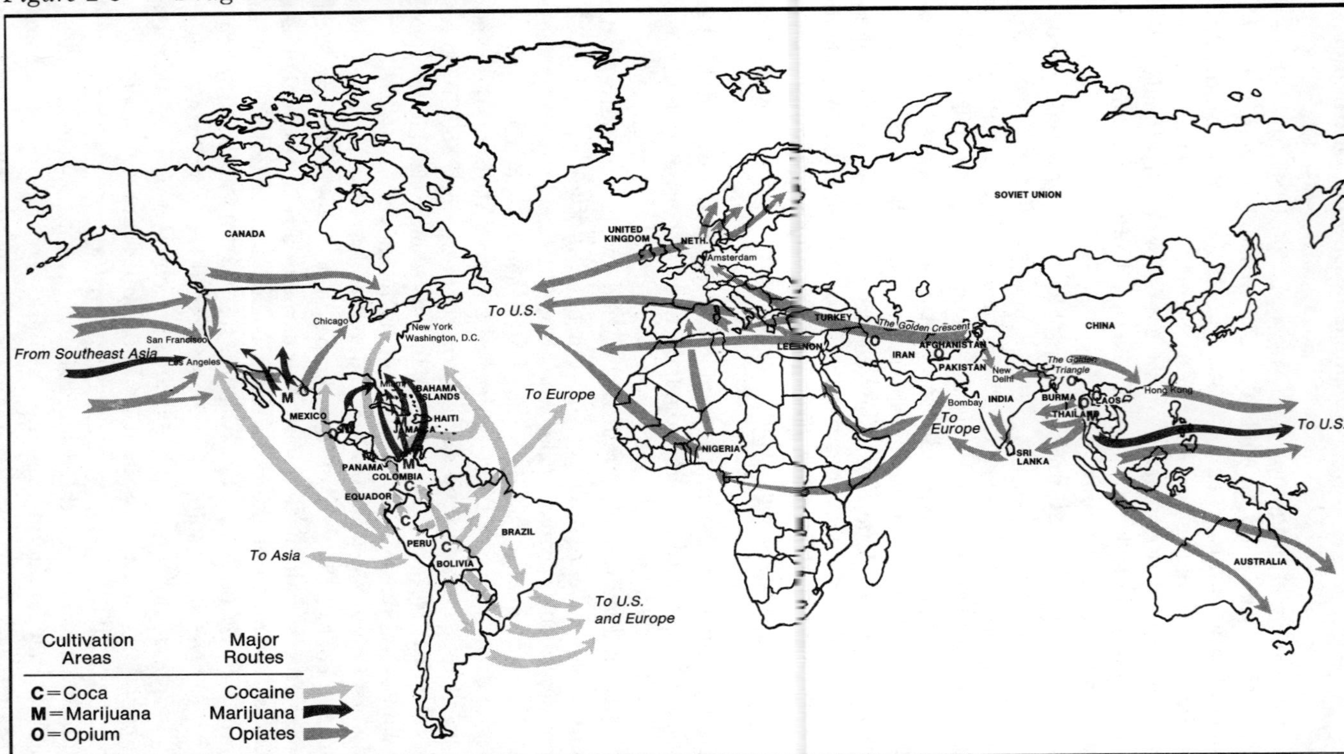

Source: Central Intelligence Agency

European Distribution Patterns

Although the United States continues to be by far the largest consumer of cocaine, taste for the drug is growing in Western Europe. To date, demand for crack is low, but Interpol, the international police organization based in Paris, reports a six-fold increase in the amount of cocaine powder seized in Europe since 1985.[14] Cocaine prices reflect the growing demand: A kilo of powder that sells for $15,000 wholesale in New York City fetches up to $40,000 in Madrid and $55,000 in West Germany.[15] The Colombian cartels have been quick to take advantage of this new export market, which they are thought to control at least as tightly as they do the North American market.

Most cocaine destined for the European market passes through Brazil, which has the highest rate of emigration to Europe of any South American nation. In part because of its similar culture and language, the Colombian drug lords chose Spain as the initial port of entry for cocaine shipments to Western Europe. Spain remains the principal gateway to the continent today. Typically, cocaine is flown from Rio de Janeiro or other South American cities to Madrid's Barajas Airport. From there, some cocaine is distributed locally, but most is shipped onward by train or car to other European cities.

As demand for cocaine has increased in Europe, however, Madrid today is frequently bypassed, and the drug is smuggled on commercial flights directly from South America to London, Frankfurt, and other cities. Little is known of local distribution networks within Europe, but the sudden increase in cocaine use in some cities provides a clue. In Naples, for example, cocaine's growing popularity is probably the work of that city's longstanding regional crime organization, the Camorra, which could easily distribute the drug through its established networks. There is some indication that limited quantities of cocaine pass through Western Europe to markets in the Middle East.[16]

Notes

1. National Narcotics Intelligence Consumers Committee (NNICC), *The NNICC Report 1988: The Supply of Illicit Drugs to the United States*, April 1989, 12.
2. Myra MacPherson, "Miami's One-Man Drug War," *Washington Post*, May 20, 1988, G1.
3. Gary Wayne Betzner testified April 9, 1988, before the Senate Subcommittee on Terrorism, Narcotics, and International Operations, chaired by Sen. John F. Kerry, D-Mass.
4. Philip Shenon, "Enemy Within: Drug Money Is Corrupting the Enforcers," *New York Times*, April 11, 1988, A1.
5. See, for example, James Ring Adams, "Losing the Drug War: Drugs, Banks, and Florida Politics," *American Spectator*, September 1988, 20-24.

6. James Greiff, "Drug Money Lurks behind Many Firms," *St. Petersburg Times*, February 26, 1988, 16-A.
7. Selwyn Raab, "Brutal Drug Gangs Wage War of Terror in Upper Manhattan," *New York Times*, March 15, 1988, B1.
8. Peter Kerr, "Cocaine Glut Pulls New York Market into Drug Rings' Tug-of-War," *New York Times*, August 24, 1988, B1.
9. Alan Riding, "Gangs in Colombia Feud over Cocaine," *New York Times*, August 23, 1988, A1.
10. Peter Reuter, *Drug Use and Drug Programs in the Washington Metropolitan Area*, Rand Corporation, July 1988.
11. Bob Baker, "Homeboys: Players in a Deadly Drama," *Los Angeles Times*, June 26, 1988, 1.
12. Quoted in William Overend, "Gang Networks Called State's Greatest Crime Threat," *Los Angeles Times*, September 7, 1988, I3.
13. See Bob Baker, "Black Gangs' Role in Drug Trade Overblown, Study Finds," *Los Angeles Times*, September 8, 1988, II1.
14. David S. Broder, "Fearing Crack Invasion, Europe Steps Up Antidrug Efforts," *Washington Post*, May 20, 1989, A15.
15. Paul Delaney, "Drug Trade for Europe Is Overwhelming Spain," *New York Times*, November 9, 1988, A6.
16. National Narcotics Intelligence Consumers Committee (NNICC), *The NNICC Report 1985-1986: The Supply of Illicit Drugs to the United States from Foreign and Domestic Sources in 1985 and 1986 (with Near Term Projections)*, June 1987, 45.

3 Competition in the Heroin Industry

Because the cocaine market is so concentrated, it would be a safe bet that the crack sold in Washington came from Peru or Bolivia and passed through Colombian hands before it entered the U.S. distribution chain. The same cannot be said for heroin. The opium poppy that is the source of heroin sold in the United States is cultivated in three major areas: the traditional opium-producing regions of Southeast and Southwest Asia and more recently, Mexico.

The three main opium-producing areas of the world together yielded some 1,500 metric tons of opium in 1985. About sixty metric tons—just 4 percent of the world opium crop—were refined into six tons of heroin and sold on the U.S. market. Worldwide demand for heroin, then, is far more widely dispersed than that for cocaine. Likewise, the industry that supplies heroin is less tightly organized than the cocaine cartels. The heroin industry's three regional branches are distinct entities with little or no overlap at the production, refining, and wholesale distribution levels. It is only at the retail level in such large heroin-consuming markets as the United States that the three enterprises enter into direct competition for street sales.

Heroin's Production and Use

Like cocaine powder and crack, heroin powder is usually refined at or near the site of cultivation. Crude opium is the dried juice of the poppy (*Papaver somniferum*), a plant that is thought to have originated in the Eastern Mediterranean and that has been grown for centuries in temperate climates of the Middle East and Asia. Opium has long been cultivated for legitimate purposes, among them the production of painkillers as well as cattle feed and fuel. Several countries, including India and Turkey, cultivate the opium poppy for these purposes. But most of the opium poppy cultivated worldwide is grown by peasant farmers for illegitimate uses.

Crude opium can be further dehydrated and concentrated for smoking, the traditional mode of administration in East Asia. Opium can also be broken down into numerous component alkaloids, notably codeine and morphine. Codeine (methylmorphine) is widely used today as a cough suppressant and mild painkiller. Morphine, a more highly addictive substance, also has found medicinal use as a painkiller. Its use quickly produces physical dependence, however, and patients who cease taking the drug experience withdrawal symptoms within hours. These can intensify for as long as two days before subsiding. Morphine's clinical use has fallen since the 1930s, when a number of equally effective, nonaddictive synthetic narcotics were discovered.

In the late 1800s a simple chemical process was developed that could transform morphine into heroin (diacetylmorphine), a highly addictive opiate, or opium derivative. Using easily procured and inexpensive chemicals such as acetic anhydride, raw opium is easily transformed into gum or morphine base and then into heroin. Today, it takes about ten kilos of opium to make one kilo of morphine, out of which an equal amount of injectible heroin may be derived. The purity of heroin sold on the street varies greatly. The drug must be "cut," or mixed with other substances, before it is taken; otherwise, it will cause poisoning and frequently death.

Mexico—First in Heroin Production for the United States

In 1987 worldwide opium production increased to meet the growing demand for heroin. The biggest increases were in Southwest Asia and in Mexico, a relative newcomer to the heroin trade. Mexico today is this country's biggest single source of heroin, accounting for more than a third of the drug available in the U.S. market. Mexican peasants began cultivating opium poppies in the 1920s to satisfy the demand of Chinese opium smokers who had settled there. But it was not until the mid-1970s that the industry took off, to fill a supply vacuum in the U.S. market left by Turkey's 1972 ban on opium production and the elimination of the heroin distribution network known as the "French connection." Until it was broken in the early 1970s, this narcotics trafficking organization based in Marseilles dominated heroin exports to the United States in much the same fashion as the Medellin cartel today dominates the U.S. cocaine market.

An aggressive opium eradication campaign conducted by the Mexican government and heavily supported by DEA had suppressed Mexican heroin production by the late 1970s. But in recent years, Mexico has again captured a growing share of the U.S. market, largely on the strength of a new heroin product introduced by Mexican traffickers. "Black tar," as it is called, is a crudely processed but potent form of heroin. It is in high demand, especially in areas of the western United States close to the Mexican border. Named for its dark color and gummy consistency, black tar is cheaper, more readily available, and purer than traditional brown heroin powder. Most heroin sold on the street has been cut with inert substances and usually is between 4 and 6 percent pure. Black tar, however, typically is retailed in uncut or lightly diluted form in the western states where it is most commonly found, and purity levels commonly range from 60 to 70 percent.

Opium poppies are grown in at least eight Mexican states. Cultivation is centered in a region that includes the states of Durango, Sinaloa, and—just south of the border with Texas and New Mexico—Chihuahua. Both brown heroin and black tar are produced in remote areas of the country in small, portable laboratories that can be easily moved around to escape detection. Mexican opium cultivators earn several times more money from their crops than their counterparts in Southwest or Southeast Asia. But because Mexican peasants have higher overhead costs than other opium growers, even these higher profits are not enough to improve their living standards. Climate and soil conditions require Mexican growers to use costly irrigation techniques. Mexican cultivators also spend large amounts of money bribing drug-enforcement agents to escape the government's aggressive opium eradication program.[1]

Largely as a result of black tar's popularity, Mexican opium production more than doubled between 1984 and 1988, from twenty-one metric tons to between forty-five and fifty-five metric tons. Once it is refined, this amount of raw opium yields between 4.5 and 5.5 metric tons of heroin. Very little is consumed locally. In contrast to other opium-producing nations, Mexico has no tradition of widespread opium use, and heroin addiction appears to be uncommon. Heroin's high price is a strong deterrent to its ever taking hold there. Mexico's opium and heroin production is thus primarily for export. About a third of this is destined for the U.S. market.

Southwest Asia's Golden Crescent

Far greater amounts of heroin are produced in the traditional opium cultivating centers of Southwest and Southeast Asia. The three main Southwest Asian producers—Iran, Afghanistan, and Pakistan—produce 1,000 to 2,500 metric tons of illicit opium a year, according to figures provided by Interpol. The border area of these three nations also is the site of the region's opium processing operations. The Southwest Asian producers sell most of their exports to Western Europe, the United States, and a growing heroin market in Africa. The Golden Crescent, as this area is known, has grown opium for medicinal purposes for centuries, but only since 1980 has it become an increasingly important source of heroin sold in the West. Today the Golden Crescent supplies nearly half the six tons of heroin marketed in the United States, 80 percent of the heroin sold in Europe, and virtually all the heroin available on the African continent.

Afghanistan

The greatest growth in illicit Southwest Asian opium production has been in Afghanistan, the region's leading producer as well as a source of heroin base and its more refined derivative, heroin hydrochloride. This land of remote mountain villages controlled by local tribes has long been an important source of opium. The government of Afghanistan provides no estimate of current opium production, but U.S. estimates place the country's opium harvest at 700-800 metric tons in 1988, compared with 400-800 metric tons the year before. According to Ramachandra Sundaralingam, Interpol's opiates specialist for Southwest Asia, the bulk of illicit Golden Crescent opium comes from twenty-seven of Afghanistan's twenty-eight provinces.

There is some dispute over the reasons for Afghanistan's leading role in the region's heroin industry. Opium poppy cultivation was banned there in 1957, and a report issued by the United Nations in 1987 states further that the Afghan government has a broad drug-enforcement program that includes "severe penalties for traffickers" and that it is "taking steps to develop prevention, treatment and rehabilitation programmes."[2]

Disputing those claims, U.S. drug-enforcement agencies assert that Afghanistan is the only major heroin-producing nation with no laws against opium cultivation and no narcotics control program. Indeed, according to the National Narcotics Intelligence Consumers Committee (NNICC), the Soviet-backed Afghan government of President Mohammad Najibullah encourages opium cultivation, as did the Soviet Union during its more than nine-year occupation of the country.[3] This official support of the industry, coupled with favorable weather conditions since 1984, explains the notable improvement in Afghanistan's opium harvests despite the crop damage caused by the war, in the U.S. agency's view.

U.S. drug-enforcement authorities feared that the withdrawal of Soviet forces in February 1989 would lead to even higher opium output in Afghanistan. As the nearly three million Afghan refugees camped on the Pakistani side of the border and the two million more in Iran return to their homeland, they will find a war-torn economy offering few profitable alternatives to opium cultivation. Poppy growers receive only a small fraction of the finished heroin's value—$60-$130 a kilo of opium, as compared with $4,000-$6,000 for the same quantity of opium as it comes out of the processing lab in the form of heroin. The contrast is even greater when heroin's street price is considered: Once it reaches the wholesale level in the United States, the farmer's original kilo of opium has multiplied in value, selling for $90,000-$200,000. At the final point of sale, it goes for $1.5-$2.5 million.[4] Afghan opium growers thus receive as little as one dollar for every $42,000 their crops bring on the retail market. But this is still more than they could make from any other cash crop.

It will take years to rebuild the orchards and vineyards that traditionally produced the bulk of the country's agricultural commodities. Moreover, the central government appears unlikely to recapture many areas held by rebel forces for some time, if at all. The continuing standoff between the government forces and the mujaheddin guerrillas means that any antinarcotics policy would not soon be effective in much of the country, especially in the main poppy-growing areas of Nangarhar province and the Helmand River valley, both near the Pakistan border.

In the State Department's view, the mujaheddin's religious beliefs preclude their direct involvement in the opium business. The agency attributes the fact that the opium trade flourishes in areas under their control to the lack of political order. Moreover, the aggressive antinarcotics program introduced in neighboring Pakistan has provided further inducement for opium cultivation on the Afghan side of the border.

Although some of Afghanistan's opium crop is consumed by the country's addict population, most is for export. The State Department estimates that 70 percent of Afghanistan's opium crop and all of the processed heroin it produces are exported to other countries in the region and to the West. Much of the Afghan opium is first transported by caravans of camels and mules along scores of winding trails through the Khyber Pass to the heroin-processing labs of Pakistan's North-West Frontier Province.

Iran

The main initial destination for Afghan opiates, however, is Iran, where members of the Baluchi tribe dominate the trade across the border with their fellow tribesmen living in Afghanistan. The profits from the sale of Afghan heroin allows them to purchase Persian carpets, canned food, radios, and other consumer items.[5] The Baluchis' trafficking operations are the latest twist in a complex history of opium production in Iran. At one time, Iran was among the world's leading suppliers of both licit and illicit opium. Under Shah Mohammed Reza Pahlavi, who was deposed by the followers of Ayatollah Ruhollah Khomeini in February 1979, the state held a monopoly over the industry. But in 1955 the rise in opium addiction among Iranians led the shah to ban cultivation and use of the drug.

At first, the ban succeeded in reducing the addiction rate, but rising opium production in neighboring countries soon undermined its effectiveness. Imported heroin, which is more compact and thus easier to smuggle across borders than raw opium, became available to Iranian opium users, further aggravating the country's addiction problem. The government tried to resolve the dilemma with partial legalization of the opium industry and registration of addicts. In 1969 the shah introduced a program of government-controlled opium cultivation designed to meet the demand for smoking opium among the country's registered addicts. Initially, Iranian opium production was sufficient to meet this demand, but by 1978 it had fallen behind domestic demand, and Iran became a net importer of the drug.[6]

The shah's opium-regulating regime was overturned by Khomeini in 1980. Today Iran's Islamic government bans the production and use of drugs, including opiates, as well as the trafficking of chemicals used in heroin manufacture. According to the NNICC, drug traffickers often are executed, and chronic abusers are banished to indefinite exile on an island in the Persian Gulf. More executions followed the introduction in January 1989 of a law that imposes the death penalty against anyone who buys or sells more than five kilos of hashish or opium, or thirty grams of heroin or other refined narcotics. However, opium cultivation still flourishes in areas of the country that are not under full government control. The cities of Tabriz and Zahedan are thought to be heroin-refining centers, and other Iranian heroin labs exist in Kurdestan along the border with Turkey.

Iranian production figures are highly speculative. U.S. authorities estimate that Iran has produced 200-400 metric tons of opium a year since 1985, a figure the Iranian government disputes. In any case, Iranian opium production is thought to be destined primarily for domestic consumption. Indeed, the addict population, estimated at up to one million, must import opiates from Afghanistan and other producers to meet the demand.

Despite highly publicized government efforts to stop the flow of drugs into the country from Afghanistan, Iran also serves as a transit point for Afghan and Pakistani opium and heroin base en route to the distribution hub of Istanbul, Turkey. Opiates are shipped in caravans of horses and mules over the mountainous, 300-mile border separating the two countries, and then processed into heroin in Turkey and other countries.

Pakistan

Although Afghanistan produces bigger opium crops, Pakistan remains a key participant in the Golden Crescent heroin trade because that is where most of the refining takes place and where the initial distribution network is based. Shortly after President Mohammad Zia ul-Haq took power in a military coup in 1977, the drug trade in Pakistan expanded to fill the vacuum left when antinarcotics crackdowns in Southeast Asia reduced supplies from that part of the world. Beginning in 1979 Pakistan also took over much of the Southwest Asian drug trade after the Soviet occupation of Afghanistan and the Islamic revolution in Iran disrupted the traditional land routes used by heroin traffickers. That same year, Pakistan instituted the region's strictest antinarcotics program. Zia banned opium cultivation, pledged to eliminate opium production by 1990, and tried to reduce the crop by spraying the poppy fields with herbicides. The program completely eliminated opium production in Malakand Agency and other traditional opium-growing areas under government control. By the early 1980s, DEA estimates, Pakistan's annual opium production had fallen from 800 tons to between 45 and 50 tons. In the mountainous areas of the northwest that are under the control of local tribes, however, the interdiction effort led to armed clashes between government troops and opium producers but had virtually no impact on cultivation.

The areas of heaviest cultivation and refining activity, in North-West Frontier Province along the Afghan border, are under the control of semiautonomous local tribes, which have successfully protected their heroin trade from government drug-enforcement activities. They have been aided by the collaboration of hundreds of thousands of Afghan refugees who fled to the province during the early 1980s to escape the escalating war against the Soviet occupation forces. Ironically, the very success of Pakistan's opium eradication efforts in the traditional cultivation areas under the government's control appears to have contributed to the recent rise in opium production in the tribal areas outside its control, as opium growers have moved there for protection. These areas now account for about half of Pakistan's opium cultivation.

Despite the government's aggressive antinarcotics control policy, Pakistan's opium crop increased in 1987 to an estimated 190-220 metric tons and remained at that level in 1988. Even so, Pakistan is now a net importer of opium because the country's one million addicts consume more opium than the country produces.[7] Most of the opium crop is processed into heroin in three areas. Khyber Agency, a region of the North-West Frontier Province that is under the control of local tribes, is thought to have about 100 labs, while Mohmand Agency and Bajaur Agency have about 50 each. In addition, some 1,000 opium-processing labs centered near Peshawar, North-West Frontier Province, receive opium gum from Afghanistan and other Southwest Asian producers. The heroin-refining business spills across the border into eastern Afghanistan's Nangarhar Province. Other facilities in southern and southwestern Pakistan along the Iranian border also produce heroin for export. The least refined form of heroin, "brown sugar," is destined for local consumption. More highly refined heroin number 3 and heroin number 4 are produced for export to Western Europe and the United States. More than six metric tons of heroin transit Pakistan each year, according to U.S. estimates.[8]

With Zia's death in a plane crash in August 1988, it remained uncertain how the government's policy on narcotics would evolve. Since she took office in December of that year, Prime Minister Benazir Bhutto has pledged to enforce her predecessor's opium ban and to expand aerial spraying to eradicate crops in previously inaccessible areas. But the center of Pakistan's heroin industry remains in the tribal areas near the Afghan border. Armed with weapons from the Afghan resistance, heroin traffickers are better equipped than ever to fend off effective government interference with their trade.

Other Countries Involved in the Golden Crescent Trade

Afghanistan, Iran, and Pakistan dominate the Golden Crescent's drug trade, but other neighboring countries also play a part. India, the world's largest producer of licit opium, harvested 600 metric tons in 1988 for pharmaceutical purposes. Although farmers must be licensed to grow the crop legally, the Indian government estimates that 10-20 percent of the opium cultivated in the country is diverted to the illicit market. In response to growing demand, more illicit opium is thought to be cultivated in areas outside those licensed for legitimate cultivation. Most of this illicit crop is thought to be consumed by domestic addicts of both opium and heroin, who now number in the hundreds of thousands. India's main role in the narcotics industry, however, is as a hub for the traffic of heroin from both the Golden Crescent (Southwest Asia) and the Golden Triangle (Southeast Asia). With the recent rise in heroin production in Afghanistan and Pakistan, much of the traffic—an estimated 30-40 metric tons a year—originates in these two neighboring countries.

The illicit drug trade thrives in countries whose central governments are weak. This has been shown in Colombia, where the cocaine barons enjoy de facto sovereignty over vast areas of the country. Similarly, Lebanon, virtually without a central government since civil war broke out in 1975, has become a small but significant contributor to the Southwest Asian opium industry. The Lebanese opium harvest, centered in the Syrian-occupied Bekaa Valley east of Beirut, grew from 3.75 metric tons in 1985 to 30 metric tons in 1988, according to U.S. estimates.[9] Lebanon also is thought to have extensive refining facilities, which are used to transform both the domestic opium crop and imported morphine and heroin base into heroin for export to the West. Egypt, which lies well outside the opium-growing region but has long served as an important transshipment point for heroin exported to Western Europe and North America, also has a sizable opium-smoking population.

Despite the traditional use of opium in Southwest Asia, heroin addiction is a recent phenomenon in the region that may be traced to the proliferation of heroin-processing laboratories set up there to meet the demand for refined heroin in the Western industrial countries. In Pakistan, where there was no heroin use as recently as 1980, heroin addicts may number a million today. Heroin addiction in Pakistan took off when that country began to take over much of the heroin-processing and trafficking side of the business in the 1980s. Because local addicts can purchase the smokable heroin they prefer close to the source, the habit can be maintained at little cost, perhaps for as little as $1 a day. Similar numbers were reported by authorities in India, where heroin addiction was also rare until recently. Farther from the processing labs, Indian brown sugar sells for about $5 a gram on the streets of Bombay, Calcutta, and New Delhi. The same quantity costs $140 a gram in Egypt, another transit country for Golden Crescent heroin where addiction has also risen.

Sundaralingam of Interpol cites two major routes over which processed Southwest Asian heroin moves from the border areas of the Golden Crescent to its destination. The traditional route, controlled by Pakistani and Indian traffickers, is through Pakistan into India and then through Europe to North America. Camel caravans transport processed heroin in large shipments, often weighing hundreds of kilos, from Pakistan to the Punjab and Rajasthan regions of northwestern India. Most of the drug that arrives in India by this route is exported by commercial aircraft. The Interpol official estimates that 30-40 percent of the heroin seized in Western Europe in 1984-86 crossed India and was flown out of the country from New Delhi and Bombay airports.

Indian law-enforcement authorities have cracked down on heroin traffic through the country. In September 1985, new drug legislation imposed ten- to twenty-year prison sentences against convicted traffickers and created special drug-enforcement agencies in Bombay and New Delhi. Drug-enforcement programs were further enhanced in 1986 and 1987, but the smugglers swiftly adapted to the sudden interdiction effort. They developed the "Balkan route" through Turkey and onward through Bulgaria and Yugoslavia into Western Europe. "Already, almost 65 percent of the heroin that comes into Europe comes on the Balkan route, a road that passes from the growing centers of Iran, Pakistan, and Afghanistan into Turkey," says Sundaralingam. Other drug shipments are carried through Syria and Lebanon along traditional overland routes or are smuggled out with cargo shipped from seaports in southern Turkey.

Turkey ceased to be a major producer of illicit opium with its highly successful ban on the crop in 1971. The ban was introduced under heavy pressure from the United States, whose large population of heroin addicts at that time obtained most of its supplies from Turkey. But Turkey is one of the few opium-growing nations that has never experienced a serious addiction problem, and the ban was lifted in 1974 to permit limited opium cultivation under government license. The crop is used in Turkey to make a variety of licit products from poppy straw, including medicines, vegetable oil, cattle feed, and roofing material.[10] The licit opium industry appears to be confined to the nine provinces where controlled poppy cultivation is permitted and to the factory in the town of Bolvadin, the only facility where poppy straw concentrate is processed for commercial use. Turkey's success in preventing illicit uses of the opium crop is due in part to the different way the plant is processed to make poppy straw concentrate, or morphine sulfate. It is illegal in Turkey to make incisions in the poppy capsule, which is the only way to extract the opium gum needed to make heroin and other opiates. To make poppy straw, the plants are left to dry in the sun, making them useless for gum extraction.

The development of the Turkish route has boosted the Middle East's role in the refining phase of the heroin industry. Syria, which has no appreciable demand for narcotics, has emerged as a key player in the region's drug business. Much of the heroin base that is smuggled through Turkey is taken over the border into the region of Aleppo in northern Syria, where it is processed into finished heroin before being shipped to Western Europe.[11] Some of the heroin base continues southward through Syria into Lebanon, which has long played a leading role in refining Golden Crescent heroin. In recent years, Lebanese refining labs have had even more business due to the increasing production of high-quality opium in the Syrian-controlled Bekaa Valley. Although the Syrian government pursues a strict antinarcotics policy, reflecting the Islamic strictures against drug use, Syrian military officers posted in Lebanon are involved in the region's heroin trade.[12]

According to Sundaralingam of Interpol, the "Turkish connection" consists of three big trafficking organizations with an extensive network of distributors and regional headquarters in Istanbul, Amsterdam, Madrid, Yugoslavia, Bulgaria, and West Germany. The three trafficking organizations draw on the large number of Turkish nationals who have emigrated to Western Europe's industrial cities since the end of World War II in search of employment. The traffickers recruit these "guest workers," who often travel between Turkey and their jobs, to transport finished heroin to market. The traffickers' job is also facilitated by the fact that many Turks living in Europe are in the trucking business and thus have access to a suitable form of heroin transport and by the relaxed customs regulations in the European Economic Community (EEC). There are no customs inspections when traveling from one EEC country to another. So, says Sundaralingam, "If a smuggler gains entrance to one EEC member nation, all twelve countries have got a problem. It is easy for these people to spread their tentacles all over." The Turkish connection now dominates the heroin traffic throughout Europe.

The heroin traffic in Western Europe has also been facilitated by the movement of large numbers of workers from opium-producing countries such as Pakistan and Lebanon to Britain, West Germany, and other industrial centers on the continent. Many Iranians also immigrated to

Europe after the Islamic revolution that brought Khomeini to power. These large expatriate communities, which often are segregated by culture and language from the European communities in which they live, provide what Peter Reuter calls "pipelines" through which heroin can pass with relatively little risk of detection to markets in Europe and North America. The heavy flow of traffic across the borders makes it hard for drug-enforcement agencies to detect smuggled drugs. Heroin traffickers can easily find couriers willing to deliver the drug to European dealers, and the emigrant communities provide natural distribution networks within the consumer countries. "The more Pakistanis resident in London, the higher the probability that a Pakistani exporter can find someone in his own community there who will know an English distributor," Reuter points out. "Thus, the number of travelers, their composition, and the size of the community resident in the user country all affect the efficiency of trafficking." [13]

Several European nations are important sources of demand for Golden Crescent heroin. According to NNICC estimates, the number of heroin addicts in Western Europe more than doubled between 1975 and 1980, when it stood at 220,000-330,000. There are now thought to be as many heroin addicts in Europe as there are in the United States, about a half million. More than three-fourths of the heroin they consume comes from Southwest Asia. Judging from the amount of heroin seized in recent years, the greatest demand for the drug is in Britain, France, the Netherlands, Italy, and West Germany. But Western Europe serves as more than a final destination for Golden Crescent heroin. Heroin-refining labs also have been discovered in Europe—four in the Netherlands and one in Switzerland in 1985, for example—suggesting that at least part of the opiate shipments to the continent are in the form of heroin base or other unfinished variants of the drug.

Western Europe is also an important transshipment point for Southwest Asian heroin headed to U.S. retail markets. The five major consumer nations play the biggest role in the intercontinental distribution of heroin. Traditionally, southern France was the center of the industry's European operations. And according to DEA, traffickers involved in the French connection who have been released from prison since 1986 are trying to re-establish their distribution network. But Sundaralingam says they have not been able to get back in business. "There is no need to reopen the French connection in Europe because heroin is already available. The Turks are bringing good stuff to the whole continent."

Alternate Routes for Golden Crescent Heroin

But the Turkish connection does not control the entire Southwest Asian heroin market. Egypt continues to serve as an important transshipment point for Golden Crescent opiates. Like many other nations that previously played only marginal roles in the illicit drug industry, Egypt has a growing problem of addiction at home. Following the sudden increase in heroin use of recent years, the Egyptian government has launched a drive against drug use and now imposes the death sentence on convicted drug traffickers.

Much of the opium and heroin traffic through Egypt is conducted by African smugglers. In Sundaralingam's view, in fact, the most enterprising heroin traffickers operating out of the Golden Crescent are Nigerian. By employing Nigerian nationals living in both producer and user countries, he says: "They control their product from its purchase in India or Pakistan, bring the stuff to Africa and then take it to Europe and the United States. I don't think any other organization covers four continents." Like the Turks, he says, the Nigerian traffickers possess the advantage of widespread expatriate communities in the main heroin markets. The large community of Nigerian traders and businessmen in India and Pakistan has allowed the Nigerians to gain control over the entire heroin market on the African continent.

Nigerian couriers have become "famous for using body cavities as a means of concealment," Sundaralingam adds. By this means each smuggler can carry as much as 800 grams of finished heroin to initial transit points in Africa, mainly Lagos, Nigeria; Abidjan, Ivory Coast; and Accra, Ghana. From there, the heroin is carried to markets in Western Europe and North America. The lure of enormous profits makes it easy for Nigerian traffickers to find couriers among their countrymen, whose standard of living has suffered because of declining oil exports and mounting indebtedness to foreign creditors. Per capita income in Nigeria stood at $370 in 1987, about half what it was in 1984. "At $2,500 a kilo for the good stuff, it's easy money," Sundaralingam notes. "If you are willing to take the heroin from Karachi Airport to Europe or America, you're a millionaire. The Nigerians don't mind getting caught."

The Southwest Asian heroin industry knows no religious or political boundaries. Not only is the narcotic cultivated and processed in areas heavily populated by Muslims, whose faith strongly condemns drug use, but it travels through the Soviet Union and other East bloc countries, whose governments have long depicted drug addiction as a curse of the capitalist world alone. Both Bulgaria and Czechoslovakia serve as transit points for heroin produced in the Golden Crescent and destined for Western markets.

The Interpol official recalled a seizure in 1986 of 220 kilos of heroin smuggled in a shipment of dried raisins and transported by truck from Afghanistan through the Soviet Union to the Baltic port of Riga, Latvia. There, the heroin was loaded onto a Soviet vessel and unloaded in

Rotterdam before it was intercepted. In addition to such evidence of a "Russian connection," the Soviet press has begun in the past few years to report a growing domestic drug abuse problem.[14] In 1988 Soviet officials acknowledged that the addict population ranged between 150,000 and 200,000 and was expected to increase as Soviet troops stationed in Afghanistan returned home. Much as U.S. soldiers who returned home from the Vietnam War were addicted to heroin and other drugs, Soviet troops are believed to have developed a serious heroin addiction problem while deployed in Afghanistan.

Southeast Asia's Golden Triangle

The Turkish connection is spreading into distribution channels in North America as well as Western Europe. But, Sundaralingam says, the Turks face stiff competition in the U.S. market from Mexican traffickers as well as from Chinese syndicates exporting heroin from Southeast Asia. Although interdiction efforts aimed at halting the Chinese narcotics traffic through Amsterdam and London have neutralized the "Chinese connection" in Western Europe, syndicates based in Thailand and Hong Kong maintain a competitive market presence in the United States for heroin produced in the Golden Triangle, an area that comprises northern Thailand, Shan State and Kachin State in eastern Burma, and western Laos. These producers, led by Burma and Laos, harvested more than 1,500 metric tons of opium in 1988 and 1989, according to State Department estimates.

The Golden Triangle's illegal drug business illustrates the similarities between the heroin and cocaine industries. Both depend on the labor of hundreds of thousands of peasants at the cultivation stage, as well as thousands more in the refining process. Like their South American counterparts, opium growers are often members of social or ethnic populations that are outside the official power structure. For them too, the main reason for growing the illicit crop is the promise of extraordinary profits. No traditional crop such as rice or vegetables yields as much cash as opium. Still, as in the Andes, even opium cultivation is not enough to bring Southeast Asian peasant farmers out of poverty. Opium growers received only about eighteen cents an hour for their labors in the mid-1970s.

Like the cocaine industry, the heroin trade offers the greatest profits at the downstream end of the business. According to a 1978 analysis, a kilo of raw opium that brought a Hmong farmer $45 at the first point of sale in northern Thailand rose in price to about $2,000 a kilo after processing into number 4 injectable heroin. By the time it was transported and sold to local consumers in Bangkok, the same kilo of heroin had more than doubled in price to as much as $4,500. But the heroin destined for export holds the greatest value added. Foreign buyers shopping in Bangkok paid $8,000-$12,000, or more than twice as much as local customers. After being smuggled into the United States, however, the same kilo of injectable heroin went for as much as $2.5 million on the streets of New York City and Washington, D.C.[15] Although these figures may have changed, the pattern of value increases they illustrate still holds true.

While it continues to be the world's largest opium producer, the Southeast Asian heroin industry has grown the least in recent years because of adverse weather conditions and enhanced opium eradication efforts. After declining in the early 1980s, though, total opium production in the Golden Triangle rebounded, aided by good weather, the use of fertilizers, and control over the main growing areas by insurgent forces. Burma led the way, harvesting an estimated 1,320 metric tons during the 1988-1989 season, up from just 350 metric tons four years earlier. The Golden Triangle shares much in common with the Golden Crescent, its major competitor. Opium cultivation is concentrated along an isolated border area, all but inaccessible to drug-control initiatives by central governments. Like the opium growers along the Afghan-Pakistani border, many of the cultivators in the Burmese-Thai border region are refugees or members of tribal groups seeking autonomy from central government rule. Above all, they all share poverty and isolation from the mainstream national economies.

Burma

In Burma, the world's leading producer of illicit opium, the official economy offers few alternatives to the heroin trade. Once the world's leading rice exporter and one of Southeast Asia's richest nations, Burma has joined the ranks of the "least developed countries," or LDCs, the World Bank's description of the world's poorest nations. In an effort to preserve the former British colony's national identity and independence from foreign influence, the one-party military regime that took over the country of about forty million in 1962 virtually closed the Burmese economy to outside trade. Controlled by state monopolies, Burmese industry and commerce have languished, and economic activity is dominated by a black market which is controlled by the country's large ethnic Chinese population. Smugglers bring in goods from neighboring China, Thailand, and India, which they exchange for Burmese opium.

The center of Burmese opium cultivation is Shan State, an isolated area controlled by insurgent tribesmen that lies along the eastern border with China, Laos, and Thailand. Shan State became even more productive as opium cultivation shifted to the region after the Burmese government

Table 3-1 Worldwide Cultivation and Eradication of Opium, 1987-1988

Country	1987 Hectares cultivated	1987 Hectares eradicated	1988 Hectares cultivated	1988 Hectares eradicated
Afghanistan	18,500	0	23,000	0
Iran	N/A	0	N/A	0
Pakistan	11,270	1,300	13,296	1,708
Total Southwest Asia	29,770	1,300	36,296	1,708
Burma	92,300	16,279	116,700	12,500
Laos	N/A	0	N/A	0
Thailand	4,674	1,740	4,604	1,761
Total Southeast Asia	96,974	18,019	121,304	14,261
Mexico	7,360	2,200	7,738	2,737
Total	260,848	40,838	322,938	34,675

Source: U.S. Department of State, Bureau of International Narcotics Matters, *International Narcotics Control Strategy Report,* March 1989.

tried to eradicate crops in the areas under its control. Before he formally resigned in July 1988 after twenty-six years as Burma's dictator, former general Ne Win used aerial spraying to destroy poppy fields, and eradicated some 16,000 hectares in 1987. His government also seized numerous heroin-refining laboratories and stepped up patrols of trails used by caravans transporting heroin out of the country.

The change in Burma's political leadership was chaotic, leaving more than a thousand dead and adding further uncertainty to Southeast Asia's opium industry. Demonstrations in Rangoon and other cities by forces that back economic reform and democratic rule were brutally crushed in a series of regime changes that culminated in a military takeover in September 1988.

The outcome of Burma's internal power struggle has important implications for the entire region. Although nearly three decades of self-imposed isolation and poor economic policy have made Burma one of Southeast Asia's poorest nations, the country boasts rich oil reserves, as well as teak, jade, rubies, and other minerals that, if efficiently exploited, could raise the country's standard of living and provide legitimate employment for much of its impoverished peasantry. But the reformers' efforts to open Burma's doors to the international economy suffered a setback with the latest military takeover, leaving few alternatives as a source of income to the heroin industry for much of the population.

Laos

Although it is a far less important producer of opium, Laos also increased its harvest in 1988-1989 to between 210 and 300 metric tons, up from 100 metric tons four years earlier. Limited opium cultivation for medicinal purposes is permitted by the Lao Peoples Democratic Republic, but according to U.S. drug-enforcement agencies, illicit opium production also is sanctioned by some officials of the communist government. Indeed, the State Department took the unprecedented step of accusing the Laotian government of trading heroin "as a matter of policy" in its August 1988 report to Congress on worldwide drug trafficking trends. The Laotian government denied the allegations.

Opium cultivation, however, long predates the current communist regime in Laos. While it was still under French colonial rule, the government established a monopoly over the opium trade, whose earnings were about a third of the colony's revenue. Until the 1970s, French-Corsican syndicates controlled the distribution of Laotian heroin to Western Europe.[16]

The U.S. Central Intelligence Agency (CIA) became implicated in the Laotian heroin trade after Laos won its independence in 1953. The CIA reportedly helped opium cultivators among the hill tribes get their crops to market as part of the agency's unsuccessful campaign to keep the communist Pathet Lao from gaining power. Today most illicit opium is cultivated in the northern mountainous areas by members of the Hmong tribe, who sell the crop to Laotian refiners. They in turn process the opium into finished heroin for export to traffickers based in Hong Kong and Thailand.[17]

Thailand

Like Laos, Thailand has a long history of opium use. Successive kings tried to curb the drug's use with penalties for both opium traders and smokers. In the mid-nineteenth century, however, the kings lifted the bans under pressure from British entrepreneurs who were eager to profit from the sale of opium to China, where the drug was legalized in 1858. As recently as the 1930s, the British were promoting the opium trade in Thailand and helped establish an area of controlled opium cultivation in the highlands, where several hundred members of the Hmong tribe were licensed to grow opium poppies.[18] In the early 1960s opium smoking was banned in Thailand, and today there is no legal production of the drug.

Thailand, the Triangle's only free-market economy and by far the richest of the three countries, has produced between twenty and forty-five metric tons of opium annually since the 1983-1984 growing season. But Thailand's role as an opium producer is overshadowed by its role as a trafficking center for the region's processed heroin. It became a major heroin trafficking country in the 1960s with the U.S. military buildup in Southeast Asia that preceded the Vietnam War. U.S. soldiers constituted a ready market for the region's processed heroin.

Refining Activities in the Golden Triangle

In addition to its leading role as a producer and consumer of smokable opium, Burma is the Golden Triangle's center for heroin refining. Usually, raw opium is transformed into *pitzu*, or morphine base, at or near the poppy fields before it reaches the heroin labs along the Burmese-Thai border. This initial refining operation reduces the product's bulk by 90 percent, making it easier to transport unnoticed. The refining side of the business traditionally has been dominated by ethnic Chinese. Typically, the border refining labs are makeshift operations, consisting of little more than a charcoal stove and a few pots, filters, and trays. Using acetic anhydride obtained illegally from India, Malaysia, or Thailand, the refiners transform morphine base into one of three products: heroin number 3, a smokable variety; heroin number 4, a 95-percent pure form that can be injected intravenously; or heroin base, an intermediate product that can be easily transformed into either number 3 or number 4 at some later point in the distribution network.

While opium smoking and chewing enjoy a longstanding tradition in Southeast Asia, heroin use is a more recent phenomenon. American military troops sent to fight the Vietnam War are said to have stimulated local demand for the drug.[19] By the time the U.S. military withdrew from the region between 1973 and 1975, sufficient demand for heroin had built within the indigenous populations of Burma, Malaysia, and Thailand to sustain the regional retail market. Addiction to heroin today is far more widespread in Southeast Asia than in the Southwest Asian opium-producing nations. The variety most commonly used in the region is number 3 heroin, or smoking heroin, a lumpy substance that contains a large amount of caffeine. Although it can be dissolved in lemon or lime juice and injected, number 3 heroin is usually smoked. Number 4 heroin, the form preferred by users in Thailand, is a more highly concentrated substance that is dissolved in water and injected. There are as many as half a million heroin addicts in Thailand alone, and another quarter million in Malaysia. Hong Kong and Burma have smaller addict populations. Injectable heroin has also recently appeared in Vietnam, where very little opium is cultivated. Finished heroin, which is used by tens of thousands of addicts

Table 3-2 Worldwide Production of Opium (in metric tons), 1985-1989

Country	1985	1986	1987	1988	1989
Southwest Asia					
Afghanistan	400-500	400-500	400-800	700-800	700-800
Iran	200-400	200-400	200-400	200-400	200-400
Pakistan	40-70	140-160	190-220	190-220	105-175
Total	640-970	740-1,060	790-1,420	1,090-1,420	1,005-1,375
Southeast Asia					
Burma	490	770-1,100	925-1,230	1,065-1,500	1,100-1535
Laos	100	100-290	150-300	210-300	210-300
Thailand	35	20-25	20-45	23-33	23-33
Total	625	820-1,415	1,095-1,575	1,298-1,833	1,333-1,868
Mexico	25-45	35-50	45-55	45-55	40-50
Total	1,290-1,640	1,595-2,525	1,930-3,050	2,433-3,308	2,378-3,293

Source: U.S. Department of State, Bureau of International Narcotics Matters, *International Narcotics Control Strategy Report*, March 1989.

in Ho Chi Minh City alone, apparently has been introduced to the country by Vietnamese soldiers deployed in Laos and Cambodia.[20]

Trafficking Patterns within the Golden Triangle and Beyond

Although both the Thai and Burmese governments have intensified efforts to disrupt the illegal opium industry, most heroin-refining laboratories in the Golden Triangle are located along both sides of the countries' common border, as well as in the areas outside the Burmese government's control in Shan State. Refiners complete the process using acetic anhydride obtained primarily from India, where it is manufactured for legitimate purposes.

The opium trade in Burma has flourished during the past four decades of civil war under the control of two main forces, the Burma Communist party and several separatist tribes concentrated in Shan and Kachin states in the north and east. Together, these forces control about a quarter of Burma's territory. Traditionally, the communist party has controlled the upstream activities of poppy cultivation and harvesting, while the Shan United Army has dominated heroin refining and initial wholesale activities in the region. Led by Khun Sa, Burma's chief opium warlord, the Shan army controlled a large area on both sides of the Burmese-Thai border until 1986, when the Thai military forced it back into Burma. Since then, disputes between these two main political forces in northern Burma have disrupted the division of labor in the region's opium industry. The two groups have divergent political goals, the communists aiming for control over the central government, the Shan militants seeking autonomy from any government in Rangoon. Still different political aims are held by a third force active in Burma's opium industry, the Kuomintang. These aging remnants of the anticommunist Chinese Nationalist forces, which retreated from China into Burma and Thailand when Chiang Kai-shek was driven out of power in 1949, once held a near monopoly over Burma's opium trade, which they used to finance arms purchases. They were driven out of Burma into Thailand and Laos in 1961. Backed by the U.S. government until the late 1960s in the unsuccessful effort to prevent the communist takeover of Laos, the Kuomintang forces based in the area have since languished, cut off geographically from the Chinese Nationalist government of Taiwan.

These widely divergent groups have controlled Burma's opium trade through a continually shifting pattern of working alliances. One recent alliance of antigovernment forces, led by the Burma Communist Party and including the Kachin Independence Army and the Wa National Army, cut off the Shan army's opium supply and took over much of its refining business. The Kachin group carved out a special niche in the business by taking control of the main smuggling route between Burma and India.

Traffickers use this route to carry Indian-produced chemicals used in refining opium into heroin across the border into Kachin State, and Burmese-refined heroin into India. The Shan army appears, however, to have held on to its dominant position in the selling of processed heroin at the wholesale level along the Burma-Thailand border.

In much the same way that the South American cocaine industry is supported by local demand among the indigenous populations of Peru and Bolivia, the heroin trade in Southeast Asia is bolstered by opium's traditional use in the region. Opium is used primarily as a recreational drug but is also widely used to treat digestive ailments and as a painkiller. Most of the Golden Triangle's opium is consumed either in the producer countries or in neighboring countries of the region. China was once a primary consumer of opium and the destination of much of Burma's opium crop when it was still a British colony. Among the region's numerous hill tribes and enclaves of ethnic Chinese, opium smoking enjoys a long tradition. Burma alone is thought to have between 120,000 and 600,000 opium addicts. Many of them are members of the Karen and other hill tribes, which include about six million people living along both sides of the Thai-Burmese border. While the tribes are not heavily involved in the production of opium, they have an unusually high rate of addiction.[21] Much smaller opium-smoking populations are found in Hong Kong and Singapore.

Ethnic Chinese operating in Burma, Laos, and Thailand control most Southeast Asian heroin trafficking at the wholesale level. Indeed, there is evidence that Chinese criminal "triads," or secret societies, maintain their control across the Pacific to the U.S. market. Triads have taken over part of the U.S. heroin distribution network that was dominated by traditional East Coast criminal organizations. As a result, the Chinese connection, which links Southeast Asian producers with ethnic Chinese traffickers in this country, has increased the Golden Triangle's share of the U.S. market from about 14 percent in 1985 to nearly 20 percent in 1986, eroding the market dominance of Mexico and the Golden Crescent.

The bulk of Golden Triangle opiates are transported from the refining labs in Burma's Shan State across the border into Thailand and on to market. Bangkok, Thailand, is the principal gateway for exports of heroin from Southeast Asia and is also an important financial center for laundering heroin profits. The product is smuggled out hidden in cargo ships, in fishing trawlers, and by commercial aircraft and also is exported through neighboring Malaysia and on to Singapore, where some is consumed. In an attempt to thwart the use of Malaysia as a transit point for the heroin trade and the growth of addiction among the local population, however, that country has adopted the most severe antidrug policy in the world, including a mandatory death sentence for anyone, including foreigners, caught in possession of more than fifteen grams of pure heroin or morphine. Between 1975 and September 1988, 73 heroin traffickers were hanged, and more than 136 awaited execution. Malaysia's narcotics policy appears to have forced traffickers to adopt alternative routes: More heroin now passes westward through India than in the past.

China is a more recent transshipment point for Golden Triangle heroin. Since 1979, the country's opening to the West has made it easier for traffickers to smuggle heroin into southern China over the land border from Burma and through Macao to Hong Kong. Despite China's strict policy against opium use, its growing volume of trade with the United States and other Western countries provides a convenient means of shipping the drug hidden away in legitimate cargo.

But stepped-up interdiction efforts have led traffickers to adopt more innovative strategies. In March 1988, Chinese drug agents intercepted almost $2 million worth of Golden Triangle heroin at a transit point in Shanghai. The narcotics had been wrapped in cellophane and inserted in the bodies of live goldfish that were to be shipped to a tropical fish importer in San Francisco.[22]

Hong Kong, whose bank secrecy laws have made it the main money-laundering center for the heroin trade in Southeast Asia, is also a major transit point for heroin shipments out of the region. A large portion of opiates shipped to Hong Kong is heroin base, which is then processed locally to make heroin 3, the variety in greatest demand by local addicts. U.S. drug-enforcement authorities estimate that half the number 4 heroin arriving in Hong Kong is then exported to the United States.

Southeast Asia seems likely to remain a major source of heroin. According to the State Department, retail prices for the finished drug were lower in 1988 than in any year since 1983, a sign that the region was producing a surplus. Further, if drug seizures in the United States are a reliable indicator of the volume of drug imports, there has been a dramatic increase in heroin imports from the Golden Triangle in recent years. Some 240 kilos of Southeast Asian heroin were seized here in 1987, more than twice the amount seized the year before. Much of the heroin from the Golden Triangle that arrives on the West Coast is then shipped to New York, where nearly half the heroin available on the street may be of Southeast Asian origin.

Heroin-Trafficking Patterns in the United States

Heroin seized in the United States is analyzed under the Heroin Signature Program, which allows the drug-enforcement agencies to trace the drug's origin and thus determine changes in trafficking patterns. In 1987, most heroin entering the United States continued to be smuggled in by passengers traveling on commercial aircraft, although the use of commercial seagoing vessels and motor vehicles was becoming more common. More than one-third of all heroin entering the United States passes over the Mexican border, mostly with couriers carrying small amounts—on average less than 400 grams—stashed in hidden compartments of cars and trucks or on their bodies. Most couriers caught smuggling black tar heroin, the NNICC reports, are illegal aliens or migrant workers who enter the country on foot and often carry the drug in body cavities or in false-heeled shoes. Black tar, whose popularity has increased the demand for Mexican heroin in the United States since 1983, was widely available in cities throughout the West by the end of 1985. Most Mexican heroin is distributed in the West and is also available in such large Midwestern cities as Chicago and Detroit.

New York City continues to be the center of heroin trafficking in the United States and is the main point of entry for Southwest Asian heroin shipped through Europe and Africa. As in Western Europe, the wholesale trade in heroin is controlled in part by resident aliens from opium-producing countries or countries heavily involved in trafficking the drug, such as Nigeria, Lebanon, India, and Pakistan. These immigrant groups compete for control over the wholesale trade of Southwest Asian heroin with traditional crime organizations in New York City, chiefly the Mafia and ethnic Chinese syndicates. From there, Golden Crescent heroin is distributed mainly in cities of the Northeast and Southeast.

The Mafia's role in the American heroin market has its roots in the crime organization's centers of activity in Italy. Italy has been an important refining and transshipment point for Southwest Asian heroin destined to both European and U.S. markets since at least the 1930s. By the mid 1960s, it was the dominant heroin trafficking organization in the United States. When the French connection was dissolved in the early 1970s, heroin processing laboratories were set up in Sicily and in the countryside around Milan in the north, employing chemists who had worked for the disbanded French organizations in Marseilles. The Italian dealers in both parts of the country import morphine base from Southwest Asia and the Middle East, chiefly Pakistan and Lebanon. According to the testimony of Tommaso Buscetta, a former member of the Sicilian Mafia who helped U.S. and Italian police uncover a major heroin distribution network between Western Europe and North America, the Sicilian branch of the Mafia has become increasingly involved in transatlantic heroin smuggling since the late 1970s.[23] His testimony is supported by DEA, which estimates that as much as 70 percent of the heroin entering this country is controlled by about 400 members of the Sicilian Mafia and their collaborators.

The Mafia has been joined in this enterprise by the two other main Italian criminal organizations, Ndrangheta, based in Calabria on the southern mainland, and the Camorra, a Neapolitan group that smuggles heroin from Naples to New York City by cargo ship. Although many U.S. Mafia families apparently continue to honor a 1957 edict against drug dealing, Buscetta's testimony led to the 1985 conviction of thirty-five American mafiosi for distributing heroin in the United States. The so-called "Pizza connection" involved a Sicilian-based operation that smuggled an estimated 1,650 pounds of heroin, valued at $1.6 billion, into New York City. There, local mafiosi sold it through pizza outlets and other small businesses in four states.

Evidence brought in the case against the Pizza connection traffickers led to an even bigger transatlantic drug bust in April 1988, which may suggest a trend toward collaboration among dealers in the heroin and cocaine industries. In this case, which then-attorney general Edwin Meese III described as "the largest international drug case ever developed by the Department of Justice," dealers exploited the cocaine glut in the United States and a similar oversupply of heroin in Western Europe to set up an unusual barter arrangement. The ring, based in Palermo, Italy, and including crime organizations in both countries, set up a cocaine-for-heroin swap that allowed them to capitalize on the distribution inefficiencies on both continents. The dealers imported cocaine from the Caribbean into the United States and then sent it to Italy by couriers, mainly women and children. There it was traded for heroin, which couriers carried to New York City for distribution there and in other U.S. cities, including Boston; Charlotte, North Carolina; Cleveland; and Los Angeles. The cocaine sent from the United States, where the drug was selling for about $20,000 a kilo, fetched about $55,000 in Europe, where demand is growing faster than the supply. In the same way, the European heroin was sold more profitably in the United States because tougher U.S. drug-enforcement efforts have driven up prices for the drug here.

New York City shares with San Francisco and Los Angeles the role of chief destination point for Southeast Asian heroin, which accounts for a growing share of the drug sold on the U.S. market. Ethnic Chinese and Thai groups, such as the United Bamboo Triad and the Four Seas Triad, two large Taiwanese groups based in California, reportedly control a large segment of the wholesale distribution of heroin from the Golden Triangle. Operating out of Chinatowns in large U.S. cities, these and other ethnic Chinese or Thai secret societies are filling the void left by the conviction of heroin dealers belonging to the Mafia and other traditional East Coast organizations. Although Chinese gangs have long been involved in street sales of heroin in the United States, they tended to buy the drug from Mafia wholesalers. But as the Mafia's role in the heroin trade has weakened, the Chinese have established their own networks all the way to Hong Kong and other export centers in Southeast Asia. This Chinese connection is responsible for the rise in Southeast Asian heroin in the United States, from about 18 percent of the total in 1987 to about 30 percent in 1988.

A case uncovered in April 1988 illustrates a typical distribution pattern for Golden Triangle heroin in the U.S. market. Chinese traffickers in Hong Kong shipped Burmese heroin overland through China and on, through Hong Kong, to San Francisco and New York City. There, ethnic Chinese gangs called the Flying Dragons, the Green Dragons, Tong On, and the Fukinbe Gang took over the drug's distribution to retailers in the Chinese communities of New York City; Newark, New Jersey; and Washington, D.C., where final retail sales were made out of Chinese restaurants.[24]

The growing influence of ethnic Chinese traffickers over the U.S. heroin distribution network during the 1980s has been accompanied by a significant change in the product's quality. The purity levels of Southeast Asian heroin available on the street have risen dramatically, affecting the average purity level of all heroin sold nationwide. Average purity in 1985 was 5.3 percent, the highest since 1977, and in 1986 it was higher still, at 6.1 percent. Since 1987 samples of the drug recovered in New York have been as much as 70 percent pure, the NNICC reports.[25] Evidence of this trend is found in the dramatic increase in numbers of heroin-related deaths and medical emergencies in New York and in other East Coast and Midwestern cities. In Buffalo, New York, for example, the number of such emergencies skyrocketed from 21 to 133 between 1986 and 1987, an increase of more than 500 percent. Less dramatic but significant increases were seen in Chicago, Philadelphia, Baltimore, Boston, Washington, D.C., and New York City.

Users of Mexican black tar appear to have learned from a similar surge of deaths caused by this potent variety of heroin when it was first introduced to the U.S. market in 1983. After rising sharply in San Francisco and Los Angeles, the biggest black tar retail markets, heroin overdoses reported by local hospitals have decreased since 1986. Because the drug is still readily available in these cities, heroin users may have learned to reduce each dose of black tar. Alternatively, dealers may be selling the drug in smaller quantities.

Heroin prices have remained fairly steady and even declined, suggesting that more of the drug is available than before, despite the crackdowns on distribution rings. The average retail price for heroin nationwide declined from $2.30 per milligram of pure heroin in 1985 to $2.12 in 1986. By 1987 the price had dropped to $2.00. Even though Golden Triangle heroin is purer than all other varieties except Mexican black tar, its cost is lower. The NNICC found that the high-purity heroin sold on the East Coast, which is predominantly of East Asian origin, ranged in price from 40 to 97 cents per pure milligram in 1987, less than half the average retail price.

Notes

1. See André McNicoll, *Drug Trafficking: A North-South Perspective* (Ottawa: North-South Institute, 1983).
2. "International Conference on Drug Abuse and Illicit Trafficking," reprint from *UN Chronicle* 24:2 (May 1987), ix-x.
3. Soviet forces entered Afghanistan December 27, 1979, at the behest of then-president Babrak Karmal to help quell guerrilla actions against his Soviet-backed government. The Soviet withdrawal, in compliance with a U.N.-sponsored agreement signed in April 1988 by the United States, the Soviet Union, Pakistan, and the Afghan government, was completed February 15, 1989.
4. Price estimates for Afghan opium and processed heroin are cited in Henry Kamm, "Afghan Opium Yield Up As Pakistan Curbs Crop," *New York Times*, April 14, 1988, A16.
5. U.S. Department of State, Bureau of International Narcotics Matters, *International Narcotics Control Strategy Report*, March 1989, 141.
6. McNicoll, *Drug Trafficking*, 34.
7. U.S. Department of State, *International Narcotics Control Strategy Report*, 153.
8. Ibid., 157.
9. Ibid., 172.
10. McNicoll, *Drug Trafficking*, 36.
11. Henry Kamm, "Drug Flow Through Turkey Defies Control," *New York Times*, July 17, 1986, A11.
12. U.S. Department of State, *International Narcotics Control Strategy Report*, 175.
13. Peter Reuter, *Eternal Hope: America's International Narcotics Efforts*, Rand Corporation, February 1985, 16.
14. See, for example, "Who Are Soviet Drug Users, Dealers?" *Current Digest of the Soviet Press*, September 10, 1986, 1.
15. McNicoll, *Drug Trafficking*, 29.
16. Ibid., 26.
17. Michael Isikoff, "U.S. Accuses Laos of Drug Trafficking," *Washington Post*, August 30, 1988, A4.
18. McNicoll, *Drug Trafficking*, 27.
19. Ibid., 26.
20. Barbara Crossette, "Addiction Rising among Vietnamese Youth," *New York Times*, April 20, 1988, 9.
21. U.S. Department of State, *International Narcotics Control Strategy Report*, 185.
22. Daniel Southerland, "Chinese Crack International Drug Ring," *Washington Post*, March 19, 1988, A15.
23. "Drugs and Sicilian Mafiosi: No Omerta Among Thieves," *New York Times*, April 1989, A20.
24. Linda Wheeler, "Asian Heroin Ring Supplying D.C., N.Y., Smashed, FBI Says," *Washington Post*, April 16, 1988, A1.
25. National Narcotics Intelligence Consumers Committee (NNICC), *The NNICC Report 1988: The Supply of Illicit Drugs to the United States*, April 1989, 70.

4 Competition for the U.S. Marijuana Market

Surveys show that fewer people smoke pot today than in the 1960s and 1970s, but marijuana is still the most commonly used illicit drug in the United States. One American in three, or sixty-six million people, reported smoking marijuana at least once, according to a 1988 survey conducted by the National Institute on Drug Abuse (NIDA) (Figure 4-1).[1] Each year, Americans spend $30 billion on marijuana, according to the National Organization for the Reform of Marijuana Laws (NORML). Drug-enforcement authorities say its supply has generally increased, from as much as 9,400 metric tons in 1986 to as much as 16,710 metric tons in 1988.[2] Not only is marijuana more widely available than ever before; it is also more potent (Figure 4-2). Using more sophisticated growing techniques, domestic cultivators are raising the potency levels of their crops.

Of all the drugs derived from cultivated plants, marijuana is by far the most versatile. The marijuana plant, *Cannabis sativa*, also known as hemp, grows under a wide range of conditions and can be cultivated almost anywhere. Unlike cocaine and heroin, marijuana requires no refining and very little handling. The leaves and flowers contain the active ingredient THC (delta-9-tetrahydrocannabinol), the weed's main psychoactive ingredient, and can be used for smoking as soon as they are harvested and dried. Marijuana can undergo a simple refining process to produce hashish (also called hash), the dried resin exuded by the plant. Sold in smokable cakes or as oil that can be mixed with tobacco, hashish is about five to eight times stronger than the flowers and leaves.

Marijuana from Latin America

Mexico and Colombia are the main sources of marijuana available on the U.S. market, and the State Department reports that both countries have increased their harvests in recent years (Table 4-1).[3] Mexican growers harvested 9,000 hectares of cannabis in 1987 and 1988, the agency estimates, making that country the largest foreign source of marijuana sold in the United States. Unlike opium and coca growers, typically peasant farmers who sell their crops to wholesalers, cannabis cultivators in northern Mexico are employed directly by the big marijuana traffickers, such as

Figure 4-1 Trends in Marijuana/Hashish Use during Previous Month by Age Group, 1972-1988

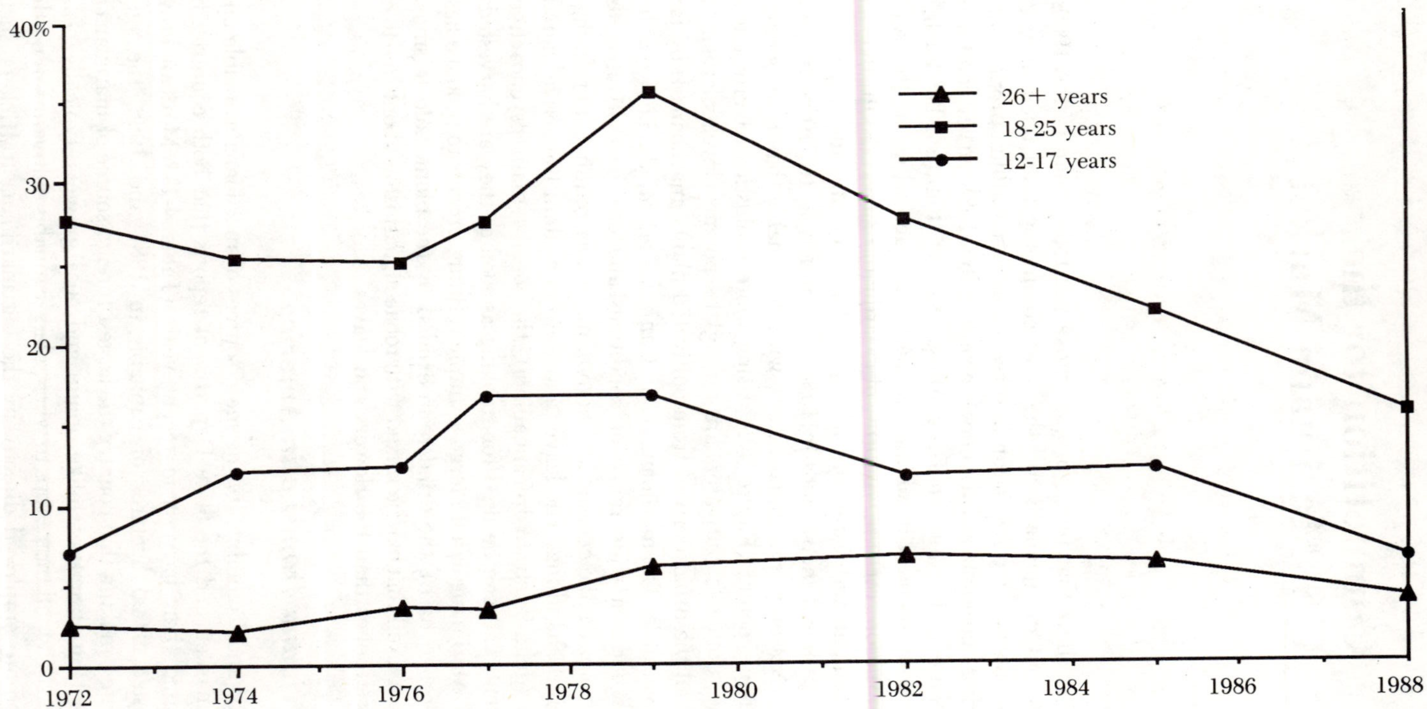

Source: U.S. Department of Health and Human Services, National Institute on Drug Abuse, National Household Survey on Drug Abuse.

Rafael Caro Quintero. One of Mexico's most notorious drug lords, Caro Quintero was charged with ordering the 1985 murder of DEA agent Enrique Camarena Salazar and is said to direct a multimillion-dollar ring that smuggles marijuana and cocaine to the West Coast of the United States. It was apparently in retaliation for Camarena's raids on Caro Quintero's large marijuana plantations in the northwestern part of the country that he was kidnapped, tortured, and murdered.[4]

The big Mexican traffickers tend to operate large agribusiness operations and control their product's distribution well into the wholesale level. They also subcontract work to small farmers throughout the country, teaching them advanced growing techniques using irrigation and fertilizers. Once largely restricted to a few areas of the country, cannabis is grown in virtually every Mexican state today. The main impetus behind the decentralization of marijuana cultivation in Mexico has been a joint U.S.-Mexico eradication campaign that since the mid-1970s has included the spraying of cannabis plots with the herbicide paraquat—a toxic chemical that can cause permanent lung damage in smokers of contaminated marijuana.

The Mexican government has recently stepped up its efforts to eradicate marijuana crops, destroying more than 3,500 hectares in 1987, up from nearly 3,000 the year before. These efforts explain the recent decline in actual yields of Mexican marijuana from 6,170 metric tons in 1986 to an estimated 4,750 in 1989, according to the State Department. Growers have tried to adapt by planting smaller crops in remote areas and by promptly harvesting and washing plants that have been sprayed with paraquat.

Although marijuana is the most widely used illegal drug in Mexico, most of the country's crop is exported to the United States. Because of the drug's large bulk, most Mexican imports are smuggled into the country by vehicle rather than by pedestrian couriers, who carry large amounts of Colombian cocaine across the Rio Grande to the North American market.

In Colombia the marijuana business pales in comparison with the huge cocaine industry. Unlike coca, which enjoys a longstanding tradition as a substance of varied uses among the indigenous people of the country, marijuana was introduced there only a few decades ago. It was the heavy U.S. demand for marijuana in the 1960s that prompted widespread cannabis cultivation in Colombia. By the early 1970s Colombia had become a major source of marijuana sold in the United States in large part because of the high quality of its product. "Colombian gold" was one of the choicest varieties of marijuana on the international market in the 1970s. And as rumors spread about the toxic effects of paraquat-tainted marijuana from Mexico, demand for Colombian gold mounted. By the end

Figure 4-2 *Trends in Marijuana Availability, Perceived Risk of Regular Use, and Use in Past Thirty Days by High School Seniors, 1975-1988*

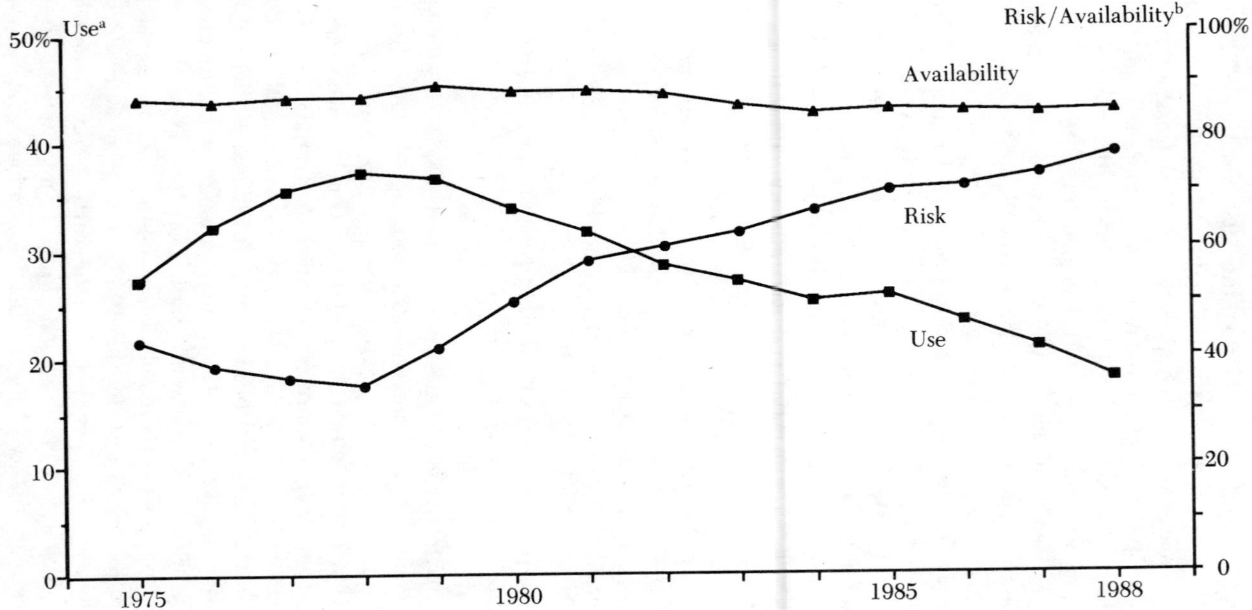

[a] Use: Percentage using once or more in past thirty days.

[b] Risk: Percentage saying great risk of harm in regular use. Availability: Percentage saying fairly easy or very easy to get.

Source: L. D. Johnston, P. M. O'Malley, and J. G. Bachman, *Drug Use, Drinking, and Smoking: National Survey Results from High School, College, and Young Adult Populations*, U.S. Department of Health and Human Services, National Institute on Drug Abuse, 1989.

of the decade, Colombia supplied 70 percent of the marijuana sold on the U.S. market. The marijuana boom employed as many as 100,000 people in northeastern Colombia and created the base for *narcotraficantes* who in the next decade would use their expertise to even greater profit in the cocaine trade.[5]

Like Mexico, Colombia has introduced aerial spraying with herbicides to eradicate cannabis plots. The decline in marijuana production in the traditional growing areas of the Serrania de Perija Mountains and the Sierra Nevada de Santa Marta in northeastern Colombia in 1985 and 1986 is attributed to these eradication efforts. But in 1988, the marijuana yield more than doubled to nearly 8,000 metric tons, as cannabis growers moved southward into the San Lucas Mountains and westward into the Darien Mountains and the Gulf of Uraba area near the Panamanian border.

Marijuana is smoked in Colombia, often as an ingredient of *bazuco*, a widely used mixture of marijuana or tobacco and coca paste or cocaine base. But domestic consumption, while on the increase, is not great enough to affect the quantities of marijuana available for export. DEA also has noted that Colombian traffickers may be stockpiling marijuana for export to the United States, which they ship on private seagoing vessels.

Jamaica and Belize are secondary foreign sources of marijuana for the U.S. market. In the early 1980s, *ganja*, as cannabis is known in Jamaica, was that country's leading cash crop and the chief source of income for at least 8,000 subsistence farmers and their families. Almost 5,000 metric tons were harvested in 1981, for a retail value of about $1 billion.[6] Although marijuana has been grown and used widely on the island for decades, most of the harvest is destined for export. The governments of both Jamaica and Belize have introduced successful cannabis eradication campaigns, diminishing their importance as sources of marijuana sold in the United States (Table 4-2). Jamaica, the State Department reports, cut its marijuana production from a high of 1,485-2,025 metric tons in 1986 to 340-470 metric tons in 1988. Jamaican posses active in the United States prefer to deal in cocaine because its more compact size and lighter odor make it harder to detect than marijuana.

But high-quality Jamaican marijuana continues to be in demand in this country. "Jamaican marijuana is considered to be of better quality, more refined, with fewer seeds and stalks," explains Sgt. Pat Moyer of the U.S. Park Police. A quarter pound of Jamaican marijuana, he says, fetches $250 on the streets of Washington, D.C., about four times as much as the standard variety. Posses control the cultivation and transport of the drug into the United States, usually in multi-ton quantities smuggled aboard noncommercial vessels, but often in smaller shipments flown in on small aircraft.

Table 4-1 Estimated Foreign Sources and Quantities of Marijuana Available for Use in the United States, 1986-1988

Country	Quantity (metric tons)	Percentage of total imports	Percentage of total supply
1986			
Mexico	3,000-4,000	37.0	30.0
Colombia	2,200-3,900	32.0	27.0
Jamaica	1,100-1,700	15.0	12.0
Belize	500	5.0	4.0
Domestic	2,100	0.0	18.0
Other	800-1,200	11.0	8.0
Gross marijuana available	9,700-13,400	100.0	100.0
Less U.S. seizures, seizures in transit, and losses	3,000-4,000		
Net marijuana available	6,700-9,400		
1987			
Mexico	3,100-4,200	37.1	27.9
Colombia	2,300-6,600	43.3	32.5
Jamaica	145-285	2.2	1.7
Belize	200	2.0	1.6
Domestic	3,000-3,500	0.0	24.9
Other			
Southeast Asia	500-1,000	7.7	5.7
Latin America	500-1,000	7.7	5.7
Gross marijuana available	9,545-16,585	100.0	100.0
Less U.S. seizures, seizures in transit, and losses	3,000-4,000		
Net marijuana available	6,545-12,585		
1988			
Mexico	4,710	34.1	25.6
Colombia	5,000-8,700	49.6	37.2
Jamaica	260-390	2.4	1.8
Belize	60	.4	.3
Domestic	4,350-4,850	0.0	25.0
Other			
Southeast Asia	750-1,500	8.1	6.1
Latin America	500-1,000	5.4	4.0
Gross marijuana available	15,630-21,210	100.0	100.0
Less U.S. seizures, seizures in transit, and losses	3,500-4,500		
Net marijuana available	12,130-16,710		

Source: National Narcotics Intelligence Consumers Committee (NNICC), *The NNICC Report 1988: The Supply of Illicit Drugs to the United States,* April 1989.

Cannabis once flourished in Belize's mountainous countryside, where favorable weather conditions make it possible to cultivate the plant year-round. The NNICC estimates that 900 kilos of marijuana can be produced from a single hectare in that Central American country. But a U.S.-assisted aerial eradication program cut annual marijuana production to just 132 metric tons in 1988. Traffickers transport the drug to the United States from Belize aboard small aircraft or private vessels.

Other Latin American countries play a relatively minor role in the U.S. marijuana market. Paraguay, which cut production by two-thirds to 1,000 metric tons from 1987 to 1989, exports most of its crop to Brazil and Argentina, where marijuana is the drug of choice among local consumers. For its part, Brazilian growers are satisfying an increasing share of the country's demand for marijuana. Cannabis is cultivated over at least half of Brazil's vast territory, most heavily in the northeastern part of the country. Brazil's domestically produced marijuana is consumed at home, and the country has not become a significant exporter to the U.S. market.

Marijuana from Southeast Asia

Marijuana production in Latin America ranged between 500 and 1,000 metric tons in 1987 and 1988, according to State Department estimates. Southeast Asian producers, who harvested a similar amount in 1987, increased their output of marijuana to between 750 and 1,500 metric tons in 1988. Although the drug is widely used in Southeast Asia for medicinal and recreational purposes, most is exported to Australia, New Zealand, and North America. Despite the Thai government's vigorous eradication campaign, Thailand is the region's biggest marijuana producer and exporter. It is also the main source of Southeast Asian marijuana in the United States, where users pay a premium for the Thai variety. Prized for its high potency, Thai marijuana contains an average 9 percent THC, about three times the average potency of marijuana available in this country. Once concentrated in Nakhon Phanom Province in northeastern Thailand, cannabis cultivation has spread to the opium-producing areas along the border with Burma, Laos, and Cambodia.

In an effort to evade aerial surveillance, farmers often cultivate cannabis with other crops. Like their Mexican counterparts, marijuana traffickers in Thailand also control cannabis production. Many of these traffickers are American, West European, and Canadian nationals who provide seeds, equipment, and chemical fertilizers to cannabis growers. Americans often control the traffic of Thai marijuana all the way to the wholesale market in networks that involve worldwide transactions. In one case, a suspected

Table 4-2 Cultivation and Eradication of Marijuana (excluding the United States), 1987-1988

	1987		*1988*	
Country	Hectares cultivated	Hectares eradicated	Hectares cultivated	Hectares eradicated
Mexico	9,000	3,750	9,000	3,997
Colombia	13,005	8,000	9,200	5,012
Jamaica	1,330	650	1,257	650
Belize	1,088	870	660	528
Total	24,423	13,270	20,117	10,187

Source: U.S. Department of State, Bureau of International Narcotics Matters, *International Narcotics Control Strategy Report*, March 1989.

American trafficker, Brian Peter Daniels, was charged in 1988 with trying to import more than 137 tons of Thai marijuana, worth almost $550 million, into the United States and Canada and with laundering millions of dollars in profits through Swiss banks.[7]

Laos and the Philippines play a lesser role in the Southeast Asian marijuana industry. Forced out by the government's marijuana eradication campaign, Thai traffickers have moved some of their cultivation over the border into Laos, where there is no eradication program. DEA estimates that cannabis cultivation in the Philippines, a key transit point in the transpacific marijuana trade, has expanded to more than half the island nation's provinces, a trend the government in Manila has been unable to stop.

Despite its high quality, relatively little Southeast Asian marijuana reaches the U.S. market. Marijuana's bulk makes it more expensive to transport and easier to detect than more concentrated drugs such as heroin, especially over long distances. In addition, the risks of interdiction are greater with marijuana than with cocaine or heroin because of the weed's strong aroma. The potential losses involved with marijuana trafficking are thus greater than they are for other drugs. American traffickers smuggle marijuana in large shipments on container ships and other commercial vessels carrying goods from the region to the United States. This is an especially high-risk way to smuggle drugs. In just one interception, for example, the Coast Guard seized a seventy-two-ton shipment of vacuum-packed Thai marijuana aboard a converted oil-rig supply vessel off the coast of Washington state in July 1988. Assuming the shipment was destined for the U.S. market, that one seizure cost the trafficker as much as $208,800,000, the shipment's wholesale value in this country, in lost revenues.[8] And that loss does not even take into consideration the cost of purchasing the drug and shipping it across the Pacific.

A Niche Market for Hashish

The impediments to importing marijuana do not apply to hashish, which continues to be supplied mainly by overseas sources. Produced from dried cannabis resin, hashish is compressed into sheets or cakes and is more easily transported than marijuana. Because of its reduced bulk and high potency, hashish offers traffickers greater profits and fewer risks of detection than the dried weed. A kilo of hashish that in the early 1980s sold for about $300 in Morocco, for example, retailed for $1,000-$2,000 in Western Europe and double that amount in the United States.[9] Most of the world's hashish is made in the Middle East and Southwest Asia, where much of the drug is also consumed.

Despite the civil war that has devastated Lebanon since 1976, the country maintains its role as the world's leading hashish producer. The center for cannabis cultivation and hash production is the Bekaa Valley, which is the country's chief opium center as well. Lebanon is also the biggest supplier to the U.S. market, though more than half of its 700 metric ton annual hash crop is exported to Egypt, and lesser amounts to other countries in the region. Lebanese hashish is also exported through Cyprus to Western Europe, where it is used as a cheaper alternative to marijuana. Together, hashish and heroin are thought to bring in as much as 20 percent of Lebanon's revenue.[10]

Pakistan and Afghanistan have produced fairly steady quantities of hashish in recent years, between 200 and 400 metric tons each between 1984 and 1987 (Table 4-3). Much is consumed locally, while large shipments are smuggled to users in India. Traffickers from all three countries control the product's distribution through Pakistan and India to outside markets, chiefly in Western Europe. Most hashish appears to leave the region aboard commercial vessels from the ports of Bombay and Karachi and overland through Iran.

India, Nepal, and Morocco are minor producers of hashish. Most of the drug produced in India is consumed locally, but that country serves as the principal gateway for hash exports from Afghanistan and Pakistan to the West.

As it is for heroin, the Soviet Union appears to be a frequently used transit point for Southwest Asian hashish. But Mikhail Gorbachev's opening to the West may make it harder for Golden Crescent traffickers to use this route. In May 1988 in the first coordinated British-Soviet drug seizure ever, British customs officials seized 3.5 tons of Afghan hashish that had been transported by rail through the Soviet Union hidden in a

Table 4-3 Worldwide Production of Marijuana and Hashish (in metric tons), 1985-1989

Country	1985	1986	1987	1988	1989
Marijuana					
Mexico	3,000-4,000	4,000-6,000	5,970-7,130	5,655	4,750
Colombia	2,000-4,000	2,530-3,630	3,435-7,760	5,927-9,625	2,090-3,395
Jamaica	625-1,280	1,485-2,025	325-535	340-470	340-470
Belize	645	550	200	120	73
Others	800-1,000	800-1,000	1,000-2,000	3,000-4,000	3,000-4,000
Total marijuana production	7,070-10,925	9,365-13,205	10,930-17,625	15,042-19,870	10,253-12,688
Hashish					
Lebanon	720	720	600	700	700
Pakistan	200	200	200	200	200
Afghanistan	200-400	200-400	200-400	200-400	200-400
Morocco	30-60	30-60	60	85	85
Total hashish production	1,150-1,380	1,150-1,380	1,060-1,260	1,185-1,385	1,185-1,385

Source: U.S. Department of State, Bureau of International Narcotics Matters, *International Narcotics Control Strategy Report*, March 1989.

shipment of licorice root, transferred to a merchant ship in Leningrad, and unloaded in London.

Hashish leaves Southwest Asia principally along the same path heroin does, via the Turkish connection into Western Europe. But there also is evidence that large distribution networks control much of the international traffic in marijuana and hashish from different producer areas to the major consumer markets. One such global ring involved a twenty-two-member organization led by Dennis Howard Marks, a British physicist who was arrested in Spain in July 1988. Marks's group allegedly oversaw the shipment of both Thai marijuana and Pakistani hashish to Western Europe and North America from its bases in nine countries.[11]

The only known exporter of hashish in the Western Hemisphere is Jamaica, where both hashish cake and hashish oil are consumed locally and exported in small amounts to the United States. Larger amounts are smuggled to Canada, where hash oil is in greater demand.

Domestic Growers on the Cutting Edge of Marijuana Production Technology

As increased interdiction has raised the cost of importing marijuana, domestic cultivators have stepped in to satisfy a growing segment of U.S. demand for the weed. About a quarter of the U.S. marijuana market is now served by American growers who are active in virtually all fifty states. Domestic growers rank just behind Mexican and Colombian exporters as the leading suppliers to the U.S. market. Domestic marijuana production took off in the late 1970s and has nearly tripled in output during the 1980s. Between 1981 and 1987 alone, DEA reports, marijuana production in the United States rose from about 2.6 million pounds to about 7.7 million pounds. NORML estimates that net profits from marijuana cultivation in the United States amounted to $26.7 billion in 1986 and $33.1 billion in 1987, making it the country's biggest cash crop.

Most analysts point to the joint Mexico-U.S. eradication program introduced in 1976 to explain the sudden rise in domestic production. As rumors spread of the potentially lethal side-effects from smoking marijuana tainted with paraquat, demand for Mexican imports slowed abruptly. At the same time, increased interdiction efforts in Florida reduced marijuana imports from Colombia and other Latin American sources. By the early 1980s the NNICC reported fewer cannabis seizures at the border. Finally, the rising demand for cocaine in the United States offered an attractive alternative for traffickers who were eager to continue tapping the lucrative North American market for drug profits.

While foreign suppliers are finding cocaine a more lucrative export commodity than marijuana, the profit motive works to the advantage of

U.S marijuana producers. This is true despite eradication programs aimed at eliminating the crop within the United States, most aggressively in California. Authorities there have concentrated their eradication efforts in the northern counties of Humboldt, Trinity, and Mendocino, known as the Emerald Triangle for their high-quality product. But cannabis is a highly versatile plant that can thrive under a wide variety of growing conditions, from the near-desert environment of the Southwest to the sub-zero temperatures of Alaska.

Intensified eradication efforts have forced recent changes in domestic marijuana production patterns. Although their distinctive lime-green foliage makes large plots of the plant visible from the air, marijuana plants can be concealed by dispersing them among other crops. Spot planting of only a few plants per plot and the irregular placement of plots in configurations known as "guerrilla patches" make the plants difficult to detect from the air. To further diminish their risk, many growers have moved their operations indoors. Although indoor cultivation is more expensive because of the necessary heating systems, special lighting units, exhaust fans, and irrigation systems, it also allows cultivators to regulate growing conditions more precisely and to produce as many as four harvests a year. In addition to hiding their activities from drug-enforcement agents, indoor marijuana cultivators can more easily protect their crops from insects and other animals as well as from "patch pirates," or marijuana thieves.

Most important, indoor cultivators are better able to produce high-potency sinsemilla, the highly prized seedless variety of marijuana developed from *Cannabis indica*, a strain that originated in the Middle East. By destroying male cannabis plants before pollination occurs, growers can stimulate THC production in female plants. This operation is easier to conduct indoors, where the environment can be more precisely controlled. Sinsemilla more than pays for the higher overhead costs of growing it, commonly fetching $165-$210 an ounce, more than twice the price charged for traditional marijuana.

It is not known how much marijuana is now produced from these indoor facilities, a sign of the growers' success at concealing their crops. DEA has estimated that only 10 to 20 percent of the sinsemilla cultivated in the United States now is grown indoors, but some of the seizures that have been made at indoor marijuana farms may provide a truer picture of their scope as well as the ingenious methods used to camouflage them. One 1987 DEA investigation uncovered an indoor marijuana plot of 1,700 plants in a large barn in the mountains of northern California. The operation included a diesel generator to provide electricity for sixty 1,000-watt radon grow lights mounted on movable tracks. In addition, the operation boasted an automatic drip irrigation and fertilization system, an air conditioning system, and other sophisticated equipment that enabled the owners to produce an estimated 5,100 pounds of marijuana each year.[12] Generators are now standard equipment in large operations because heavy energy requirements for indoor cultivation make it easy for drug-enforcement authorities to trace big indoor pot farms through utility companies.

Marijuana growers recently have adopted another way to offset the risks of detection. Since the passage of a 1984 anticrime bill, convicted growers frequently must forfeit their land, buildings, and other property. To avoid this risk, many have moved their outdoor plots to federal property such as the national forests, which also present the advantage of being situated in remote, sparsely populated areas of the country. The U.S. Forest Service estimates that nearly 8,000 marijuana operations had shifted to national forest land by 1986, especially in Washington, Oregon, and California. "Today cannabis production in the National Forests is a major billion dollar industry," said William L. Rice, deputy chief for administration of the Forest Service, a branch of the Department of Agriculture.[13] Rice said that since 1981, more than 1.3 million cannabis plants, worth at least $2.5 billion, had been destroyed on national forest lands. Because the authorities seize only an estimated 40 percent of the total, the value of marijuana grown on federal property probably exceeds $5 billion.

Rice also noted that most of the small, independent growers who dominated the marijuana industry in the early 1970s have been replaced by large commercial enterprises, most notably in the Western states, where sinsemilla growers have transformed their plantations into less easily detectable "cluster" sites on national forest land. These newer enterprises often are financed by urban investors, Rice said, who hire armed guards and laborers to protect and tend the crops.

As domestic marijuana has risen in quality and value, growers have adopted more aggressive tactics to defend their crops. In addition to poisons designed to kill animals that eat cannabis, growers often set up dangerous booby traps, complete with trip wires that set off grenades or shotguns, especially during the harvest season in September and October. But recently, growers have started guarding their plots for longer periods. "There is considerable activity at the sites from February through October," Rice said, "including site preparation, transplanting, developing watering systems, plant sexing, pruning, harvesting, drying, and transportation out of the forest." As a result, the Forest Service has closed to the public nearly 900,000 acres of park land, chiefly in California and in Hawaii Volcanoes National Park.

The risk of detection may seem slight when compared with the profits to be gained from marijuana production. When cannabis is sown outdoors and cultivated the same way as corn or wheat, the cost of producing a pound of finished marijuana may average about $200. If it is germinated and grown indoors, the cost doubles, to about $400. But once it reaches the wholesale level, each cultivated cannabis plant brings the grower a profit of 100 to 400 percent.[14] With profits of this magnitude, it is not surprising that marijuana cultivation appeals to others besides major traffickers. American farmers, caught in a financial squeeze by drought and low grain prices, have been lured by the lucrative marijuana trade. In one celebrated case, a rancher in northern Montana sold nearly a half million dollars worth of marijuana in an effort to stave off bankruptcy. While they continued to grow their traditional grain crop, Richard Kurth and his family supplemented their income for two years by growing marijuana in barns on the ranch before they were discovered.[15]

The Drug Enforcement Agency estimates that as much as 8,300 metric tons of cannabis were produced domestically last year, though eradication lowered the amount available for consumption to 3,000 tons. While drug-enforcement agents eradicated more than seven million plants in forty-six states in 1987, their efforts had little impact on marijuana availability. Seven states—California, Hawaii, Kansas, Kentucky, Louisiana, Missouri, and Tennessee—are the primary domestic producers of marijuana, accounting for 79 percent of total production. Unlike the subsistence farmers who barely eke out a living from cultivating coca bushes or opium poppies, American marijuana growers are often employed, middle-income individuals who cultivate cannabis as a profitable side enterprise. Unconstrained by poverty, domestic marijuana growers have been able to increase productivity since the early 1980s, despite stepped-up eradication efforts, by adopting innovative farming techniques, such as indoor cultivation and hydroponics. Almost half the domestic marijuana crop produced today is sinsemilla, much of which is cultivated indoors.

Whereas Colombian marijuana has an average THC content of 3-6 percent, sinsemilla's potency is 8 percent or higher. This improvement in the quality and potency of domestically produced marijuana has driven up the price as well (Table 4-4). While Colombian marijuana was the product of choice in the early 1980s and sold for as much as $1,000 for 500 grams, the same amount of domestic marijuana went for just $200 to $300.[16] Today marijuana consumers are more likely to buy American. Sgt. Moyer says that a one-gram bag of high-grade domestic sinsemilla sells for as much as $10 today, up from $5 per four-gram bag just a few years ago.

Yet another key ingredient in domestic marijuana's profitability is the relatively low risk involved in producing and selling the drug. Although some states, especially California, have instituted aggressive cannabis eradication campaigns, few areas fall under the degree of scrutiny by drug-enforcement agencies that prevails at the border. Because domestic cannabis growers do not risk detection at the border, their distribution costs are lower. Domestic sinsemilla, initially sold in twenty- to fifty-pound

Table 4-4 Marijuana Trafficking Indicators, 1985-1988

Prices	1985	1986	1987	1988
Commercial grade				
Wholesale (pound)	$300-$600	$350-$700	$350-$1,450[a]	$350-$1,800[a]
Retail (ounce)	$50-$100	$45-$120	$60-$130	$30-$250
Potency (THC)[b]	3.70%	3.34%	3.46%	3.63%
Sinsemilla				
Wholesale (pound)	$1,200-$2,500	$800-$2,000	$1,400-$2,100	$800-$3,000
Retail (ounce)	$120-$200	$100-$200	$160-$210	$120-$300
Potency (THC)[b]	7.28%	8.44%	7.97%	8.43%

[a] The wide range reflected temporary shortages in some reporting areas.
[b] THC (delta-9-tetrahydrocannabinol) is the principal psychoactive ingredient in cannabis.

Source: National Narcotics Intelligence Consumers Committee (NNICC), *The NNICC Report 1988: The Supply of Illicit Drugs to the United States*, April 1989.

bundles, changes hands as few as two or three times from the farm to the street, says Peter Reuter of the Rand Corporation. "It may turn out, unfortunately, that the United States has at last managed (rather expensively) to provide effective tariff protection for one industry: marijuana production."[17]

Notes

1. National Institute on Drug Abuse, *1988 National Survey on Drug Abuse*, August 1989.
2. National Narcotics Intelligence Consumers Committee (NNICC), *The NNICC Report 1988: The Supply of Illicit Drugs to the United States*, April 1989, 6-7.
3. U.S. Department of State, Bureau of International Narcotics Matters, *International Narcotics Control Strategy Report*, March 1989, 10.
4. Three men have been convicted of complicity in the murder of Camarena and his pilot, Alfredo Zavala Avelar, whose mutilated bodies were found buried near Guadalajara on March 5, 1985.
5. Bruce M. Bagley, "Colombia and the War on Drugs," *Foreign Affairs* (Fall 1988): 74.
6. André McNicoll, *Drug Trafficking: A North-South Perspective* (Ottawa: North-South Institute, 1983), 55.
7. John Parry, "Swiss Arrest Suspected Marijuana Kingpin," *Washington Post*, October 8, 1988, A27.
8. This figure is extrapolated from the NNICC's 1987 marijuana price tables.
9. McNicoll, *Drug Trafficking*, 59.
10. E. A. Wayne, "Militias Cooperate on Drug Trade to Pay for War—Against Each Other," *Christian Science Monitor*, March 9, 1988, 1.
11. Michael Isikoff, "Global Drug-Smuggling Ring Is Broken, U.S. Officials Say," *Washington Post*, July 26, 1988, A6.
12. U.S. Congress, House, Committee on Government Operations, H.R. 100-454, *Going to Pot: Marijuana Cultivation on Public Lands and the Federal Response*, 100th Cong., 1st sess., November 20, 1987, 17.
13. Rice testified May 12, 1988, at hearings before the House Government Operations Subcommittee on Government Information, Justice and Agriculture.
14. House Committee on Government Operations, *Going to Pot*, 13.
15. "Illicit Crop Almost Saved Farm; Town Now Split," *New York Times*, September 7, 1988, A24.
16. McNicoll, *Drug Trafficking*, 49.
17. Peter Reuter, Gordon Crawford, and Jonathan Cave, *Sealing the Borders: The Effects of Increased Military Participation in Drug Interdiction* (Santa Monica, Calif.: Rand Corporation, 1988), 127.

5 U.S. Self-Sufficiency in "Dangerous Drugs"

There is one class of illegal drugs sold on the U.S. market whose production and distribution are almost completely confined to the United States. Grouped into a category the Drug Enforcement Agency calls "dangerous drugs," these substances generally are or were at one time available by prescription. They are either diverted from their legitimate use through unscrupulous physicians or pharmacy burglaries or produced illicitly in clandestine laboratories around the country. Some "dangerous drugs" are widely distributed—the prescription tranquilizer Valium (diazepam), for example, is one of the most widely abused drugs in the country. But the use of most dangerous drugs is less evenly distributed than other illegal drugs and tends to be concentrated in certain urban areas.

Among the most commonly abused dangerous drugs are lysergic acid diethylamide (LSD), phencyclidine (PCP), methamphetamine, Valium, and so-called designer drugs, clandestinely produced substances that are chemically similar to other drugs of abuse, but often more potent. Several classes of dangerous drugs are distinguished by their chemical properties and their effects on the user. Stimulants, whose effects of excitement and euphoria are similar to those of cocaine, include amphetamines such as methamphetamine. Once used in diet pills to reduce appetite, the legal uses of these drugs now are confined to the treatment of juvenile hyperactivity and narcolepsy. Synthetic narcotics or analgesics were developed in the 1930s as nonaddictive alternatives to opiates for use as painkillers. The best-known hallucinogenic or psychotomimetic drugs, apart from marijuana and hashish, are LSD and PCP. Another class of dangerous drugs includes barbiturates and related substances whose sedative or depressant effects are similar to those of alcohol.

Dangerous drugs are produced throughout much of the world and are frequently diverted from their legitimate channels of distribution. Because these substances have lawful uses, smugglers find it relatively easy to transport them across borders; falsified import documents are generally all that is necessary. But unlike cocaine, heroin, and marijuana, most dangerous drugs sold on America's streets are made in the United States.

In recent years, most seizures of dangerous drugs have involved amphetamines, stimulants produced both legally for medicinal purposes and illegally in clandestine labs. Methamphetamine, also known as speed or crystal, has been increasingly available since the beginning of the decade, when clandestine laboratory operators first discovered a simple chemical process known as ephedrine reduction to produce the drug. Methamphetamine production is centered in San Diego, but clandestine labs are also active in other cities in California, as well as in Oregon, Washington, and Texas despite laws recently enacted in those states to restrict the availability of ephedrine and other chemicals used to produce the drug. Motorcycle gangs based in Los Angeles have long dominated the production and distribution of methamphetamine, especially in western and southwestern states where demand for the drug is concentrated.[1]

The late 1980s have seen a rise in the use of another amphetamine, MDMA, also known as XTC or Ecstasy. A combination of amphetamine and the hallucinogen mescaline sold as tablets or capsules, Ecstasy is in greatest demand among college students and recent graduates. The hottest markets for the drug, the National Narcotics Intelligence Consumers Committee (NNICC) reports, are the metropolitan areas of New York City, Atlanta, Miami, Chicago, Denver-Boulder, Dallas, and Houston.[2]

Most other dangerous drugs are made available by a variety of sources, and demand for different types of drugs fluctuates from year to year. Use of LSD, the hallucinogen that was the hallmark of an entire generation during the late 1960s and early 1970s, fell after widely publicized cases of injury and death caused by the drug. Although the NNICC has reported a rise in the use of LSD since 1987, the dosage units generally sold—20-80 micrograms—are only one-half to one-fifteenth the potency of those available in the late 1960s and early 1970s. The production and distribution of LSD throughout the United States is still controlled by a small number of groups based in northern California.

While demand for LSD and PCP has risen, the use of depressants such as methaqualone and diazepam has declined since the early 1980s. Further, demand for these substances varies from city to city. For example, methaqualone, a synthetic depressant sold under the brand names Quaalude and Mandrax, was widely available in New York City in the early 1980s, but seems no longer to be in great demand there. Quaalude is harder to obtain as a result of international controls on the drug's availability and a 1984 law making its possession illegal in the United States except for research purposes. Although the drug is still used in many countries as a sedative and hypnotic agent, stockpiles kept for these legitimate medical uses have largely been kept out of the hands of traffickers. They have reacted to the scarcity of methaqualone by producing look-alike drugs containing different depressant agents such as diazepam and phenobarbital, which dealers then sell on the street as Quaalude or Mandrax. Most of these counterfeit products, like true methaqualone, are smuggled into the United States from Canada and Mexico.

Like Quaalude, Preludin, a prescription diet pill popular in Washington, D.C., in the early 1980s, has virtually disappeared from the local market. But a more dangerous substance, the hallucinogen PCP, has remained a favorite drug in the Washington area for the past decade. Unlike cocaine, which produces an intense but brief period of euphoria, the effects of PCP can last for hours or even days. Because the chemical is stored in the body's fatty tissues, the PCP user can experience a sudden rush when the substance re-enters the bloodstream long after taking the drug. "Loveboat," a popular mixture of PCP and marijuana, can be lethal.

Originally produced as an anesthetic for veterinary use, PCP was taken off the market when its hallucinogenic qualities were discovered. Today illicit production of the highly volatile liquid is centered in Los Angeles, where much of it is also consumed. But most PCP is shipped to the East Coast. Although it has not figured as a center for PCP manufacture since 1982, when a special police task force expelled local clandestine labs, Washington, D.C., remains the principal distribution hub for the U.S. PCP industry. Since 1983, sales of the drug to local consumers have escalated faster than in any other market despite a fall in local demand for the drug in 1988 when many drug users switched to crack. Secondary markets for PCP include Baltimore, San Francisco, St. Louis, Chicago, New Orleans, and New York City.

Enormous profits can be made all along the PCP distribution chain from the lab to the consumer. According to one drug-enforcement agent, a gallon of PCP today costs about $500 in chemicals to make and can sell for as much as $15,000. Distributors then sell the PCP in one-ounce amounts—commonly in vanilla extract bottles—for $250-$300 each to street dealers, for a further markup of more than 100 percent. Dealers who buy the one-ounce bottles treat plant material—parsley or, in the case of loveboat, marijuana—which they sell on the street in four- or five-ounce tins. Each vanilla extract bottle holds enough PCP to treat about eighty-four tins, which sell in Washington, D.C., for $10-$15 apiece. Even allowing for the cost of parsley and aluminum foil, the street dealer can clear nearly $1,000 in profit from a single ounce of PCP. There is also a brisk trade in ready-to-use "dippers," cigarettes that have been saturated with PCP and sell for $25-$30 each (Table 5-1).

Narcotic or analgesic substances such as Percodan (oxycodone) and Dilaudid (hydromorphone) often are used by heroin addicts, both as substitutes for and as supplements to heroin. Although hydromorphone use has declined since the mid-1980s nationally, Washington, D.C., remains an active market for the drug. Unlike heroin, Dilaudid is water-soluble and does not need to be heated before injection. "You just grind it up and shoot

Table 5-1 Selected Dangerous Drugs Trafficking Indicators, 1985-1988

Prices	1985	1986	1987	1988
Wholesale				
Amphetamine (dosage unit)	$1.50	$1.50	$1.50	$1.50
Methamphetamine (ounce)	$800-$2,000	$1,000-$1,800	$1,000-$1,500	$700-$1,800
Methaqualone (dosage unit)	$0.50-$2.00	$0.50-$2.00	$0.50-$2.00	$0.50-$2.00
PCP (ounce)	$950-$1,100	$950-$1,100	$975-$1,100	$1,000-$1,200
LSD (dosage unit)	$1.50	$1.00-$2.30	$0.75-$3.00	$0.35-$1.50
Retail				
Amphetamine (dosage unit)	$3.00	$3.00	$3.00	$3.00
Methamphetamine (gram)	$60-$100	$60-$120	$60-$120	$60-$125
Methaqualone (dosage unit)	$3.00-$10.00	$3.00-$10.00	$3.00-$10.50	$3.00-$10.50
PCP (1 cigarette)[a]	N/A	$30-$50	$30-$70	$30-$70
LSD (dosage unit)	$2.00-$5.00	$3.00-$6.00	$2.00-$8.00	$2.00-$8.00
Hydromorphone (4 milligrams) (Dilaudid)	$50	$30-$65	$20-$60	$20-$80

[a] A full-length cigarette saturated with PCP and sold in Los Angeles.

Source: National Narcotics Intelligence Consumers Committee (NNICC), *The NNICC Report 1988: The Supply of Illicit Drugs to the United States*, April 1989.

it," Sgt. Pat Moyer says. "You can dissolve it and inject it in the time it takes to stop for a traffic light." Unlike most banned substances, Moyer says, Dilaudid is used almost exclusively by young, lower-middle-class white males who buy the drug from their vehicles along a few well-defined blocks of the city. Because the local market for Dilaudid is so narrow, fluctuations in demand for the drug within this restricted group have a noticeable impact on retail prices. As demand for Dilaudid increased faster than the drug's availability, its street price rose abruptly from $40 a dosage unit in 1984 to as much as $65 in 1986.[3] As the drug became more available the price fell back and now stands at $35-$40 per dose.

Designer drugs have become popular alternatives to many banned substances in the 1980s. Chemically similar to the drugs they are made to resemble, they closely reproduce the effects of heroin, cocaine, and other illegal substances. Although these chemical substitutes also were banned under the Anti-Drug Abuse Act of 1986, they continue to be a major component of the traffic in dangerous drugs. Their distribution is far less widespread than that of cocaine or heroin, but in some cases they are among the most dangerous substances on the illicit market. Those mimicking the effects of narcotics, such as fentanyl analogues, have been found to be more than 1,000 times as potent as morphine and have caused more than 100 deaths by overdose.[4]

Notes

1. National Narcotics Intelligence Consumers Committee (NNICC), *The NNICC Report 1988: The Supply of Illicit Drugs to the United States,* April 1989, 55-56.
2. Ibid., 59.
3. National Narcotics Intelligence Consumers Committee (NNICC), *The NNICC Report 1985-1986: The Supply of Illicit Drugs to the United States from Foreign and Domestic Sources in 1985 and 1986 (with Near Term Projections),* June 1987, 60.
4. National Narcotics Intelligence Consumers Committee (NNICC), *The NNICC Report 1987: The Supply of Illicit Drugs to the United States,* April 1988, 51.

6 The Effects of Drug Use on American Society

The international business of illicit drugs described in the preceding chapters is a highly diverse industry. Most drugs are produced in several countries; some, especially cocaine, are products of efficient industries whose leaders have established near-monopolies over their sectors of the business. The heroin industry is the most competitive, as worldwide production is somewhat evenly divided among three blocs of producers. Marijuana production is among the least structured segments of the illicit drug industry; pot producers are widely dispersed both globally and within national boundaries. Although there is recent evidence of market concentration among domestic producers, no U.S. counterpart in marijuana production and marketing exists to compare with the Colombian cartels that appear to control virtually the entire movement of cocaine from cultivation to final sale.

Linking all these product segments of the drug industry is the market. Like foreign manufacturers of automobiles, electronic goods, and other consumer items, illicit drug producers throughout the world look to the United States as the primary destination for their products. While nearly all drug producers reserve some of their goods for sale at home, in neighboring countries, and in other overseas markets such as Western Europe, the health of their business is vitally linked to the demand for their products in the United States.

Patterns of Drug Use

Statistics indicate that, on the whole, business has never been better. It is true that the National High School Survey shows a decline in the use of certain drugs by American teenagers currently enrolled in high school (Table 6-1). It was these data that led President Ronald Reagan to declare in early 1988 that his administration's war on drugs was nothing less than "an untold American success story" and that "our students are just saying 'no' to drugs."[1]

But the high school survey tells only part of the story. It does not include high school dropouts who are thought to account for a large portion of the drug-using population. The other main barometer of the industry's health,

Figure 6-1 Weekly Use Among Cocaine Users, 1985-1988

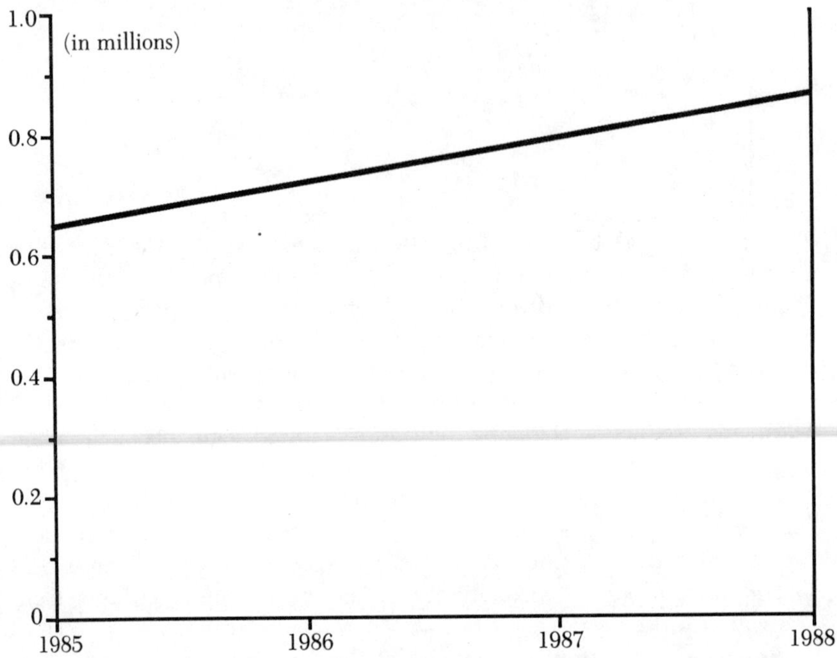

Source: U.S. Department of Health and Human Services, National Institute on Drug Abuse.

the National Institute on Drug Abuse's (NIDA) National Household Survey on Drug Abuse, paints a far more discouraging picture of drug use in the United States during the 1980s. The 1985 survey showed that overall use of illicit drugs had fallen from the late 1970s to 1985, but that demand remained high (Figures 6-1 and 6-2). NIDA estimated at mid-decade that twenty-three million Americans, about one in ten, used illegal drugs at least once a month.[2]

As the death toll from drug dealers' turf wars rose in 1988 the Reagan administration had to eat its words. In 1988 illicit drugs rose to the top of the list of public concerns in poll after poll, a trend that was reflected in the political exchanges of that election year. Officials argued over new weapons to destroy the narcotics industry, including use of the military to seize drugs on their way to the U.S. market, extensive drug testing of both government and private sector workers, and bureaucratic changes to better coordinate the efforts of the agencies involved in drug enforcement. As its final act before adjourning in October 1988, the 100th Congress approved massive antidrug legislation, while the candidates for the presidency argued over who would be tougher on drugs if elected.

Figure 6-2 Number of Cocaine Users during Previous Year, 1985-1988

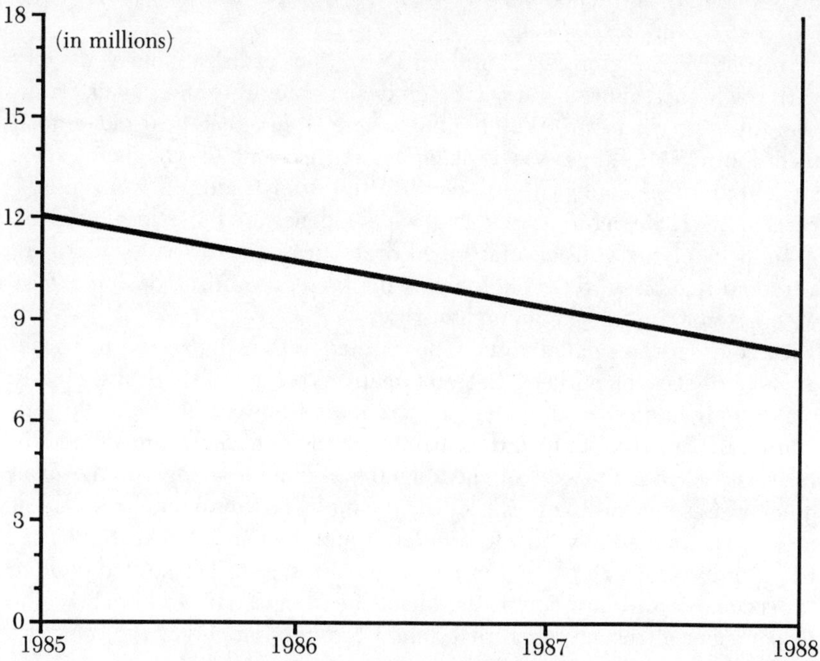

Source: U.S. Department of Health and Human Services, National Institute on Drug Abuse.

A more recent edition of NIDA's household survey, while showing a fall in demand for illegal drugs among casual users, indicates the emergence of a growing class of hard-core users of highly addictive substances including crack.[3]

Crime and the Drug Market

While the surveys show little change in Americans' taste for illicit drugs, several new trends in the drug market help explain the antidrug furor unleashed in the late 1980s. The most evident is mounting crime linked mainly to the sale of crack cocaine. From the wholesale level to the street, the crack trade has been accompanied by unprecedented violence associated with the sale of illicit substances. This is due to the marketing techniques used by crack's dominant traffickers, the Jamaican posses, and, at least to some extent, well-organized gangs of youths based in Los Angeles and now present in most cities where crack is in greatest demand. Homicide rates in many cities across the country, from New York City to Los Angeles, have skyrocketed, and police officials attribute most of the killings to the crack trade. Most of the victims are drug dealers and runners who die in gun fights over control of street-corner retail sites or crack houses. But drug-related killings increasingly are claiming the lives of innocent bystanders as well.

In 1988 Washington, D.C., nudged Detroit out of its ranking as the city with the highest murder rate, as crack dealers fought to stake their claims over drug markets. In Washington, where a nineteen-year-old annual record of 287 killings was broken before the end of October, police attributed 70 percent of the slayings to the drug trade, up from just 17 percent in 1985 before crack had widely penetrated the local market. Assaults involving guns also increased dramatically in the nation's capital, a trend officials said reflected the growing presence of drug dealers armed with automatic and semiautomatic rifles.

Of course, drug-related crime is not limited to the slayings in turf battles among street-level pushers. Users of many types of illicit drugs, chiefly such highly addictive substances as heroin, and now crack, typically turn to criminal activities to feed their habits. Although a single dose of crack is relatively cheap, the cost of meeting the addict's craving for the drug quickly rises beyond the means of the unemployed youth and young adult users, who increasingly turn to crime to support their habit. In New York City, for example, 80 percent of the people arrested in 1986 tested positive for cocaine use, almost double the incidence found in 1984.[4] Similarly, the Department of Justice found that almost half the inmates of the country's state prisons who were serving time for robbery or burglary were under the influence of an illegal drug at the time they committed the crime.[5] Given their chronic need for cash, many who use drugs are repeat offenders. The statistics are sketchy, but anecdotal evidence provides a clue to the extent of the problem. One suspect in Hartford, Connecticut, admitted to committing 600 burglaries over a two-year period to sustain his $300-a-day cocaine habit.[6]

Justice System Overload

Drug arrests have flooded the criminal justice system, creating backlogs in the courts and severe prison overcrowding. Responding to the court overflow, officials are streamlining the criminal justice process in drug cases. In New York, for example, there now are special narcotics sections that deal only with drug-related cases. Instead of following the normal procedure of indictment, arraignment, and hearings leading to a guilty plea or trial by jury, a process that can take months, drug suspects commonly are offered a plea bargain. In exchange for pleading guilty, defendants generally receive lighter sentences than if they were convicted at trial, while the criminal justice system avoids complete breakdown from the flood of drug arrests. Whether society as a whole profits by such streamlining, however, is doubtful: Dealers who accept the plea bargain

Table 6-1 Percentage of High School Seniors Who Have Ever Used Drugs, 1975-1988

	1975	1976	1977	1978	1979	1980	1981	1982	1983	1984	1985	1986	1987	1988
Marijuana/Hashish	47.3	52.8	56.4	59.2	60.4	60.3	59.5	58.7	57.0	54.9	54.2	50.9	50.2	47.2
Inhalants	N/A	10.3	11.1	12.0	12.7	11.9	12.3	12.8	13.6	14.4	15.4	15.9	17.0	16.7
Inhalants adjusted[a]	N/A	N/A	N/A	N/A	18.2	17.3	17.2	17.7	18.2	18.0	18.1	20.1	18.6	17.5
Amyl & butyl nitrites	N/A	N/A	N/A	N/A	11.1	11.1	10.1	9.8	8.4	8.1	7.9	8.6	4.7	3.2
Hallucinogens	16.3	15.1	13.9	14.3	14.1	13.3	13.3	12.5	11.9	10.7	10.3	9.7	10.3	8.9
Hallucinogens adjusted[b]	N/A	N/A	N/A	N/A	17.7	15.6	15.3	14.3	13.6	12.3	12.1	11.9	10.6	9.2
LSD	11.3	11.0	9.8	9.7	9.5	9.3	9.8	9.6	8.9	8.0	7.5	7.2	8.4	7.7
PCP	N/A	N/A	N/A	N/A	12.8	9.6	7.8	6.0	5.6	5.0	4.9	4.8	3.0	2.9
Cocaine	9.0	9.7	10.8	12.9	15.4	15.7	16.5	16.0	16.2	16.1	17.3	16.9	15.2	12.1
Crack	N/A	N/A	N/A	N/A	N/A	N/A	N/A	N/A	N/A	N/A	N/A	N/A	5.6	4.8
Other cocaine	N/A	N/A	N/A	N/A	N/A	N/A	N/A	N/A	N/A	N/A	N/A	N/A	14.0	12.1
Heroin	2.2	1.8	1.8	1.6	1.1	1.1	1.1	1.2	1.2	1.3	1.2	1.1	1.2	1.1
Other opiates[d]	9.0	9.6	10.3	9.9	10.1	9.8	10.1	9.6	9.4	9.7	10.2	9.0	9.2	8.6
Stimulants[d]	22.3	22.6	23.0	22.9	24.2	26.4	32.2	35.6	35.4	N/A	N/A	N/A	N/A	N/A
Stimulants adjusted[c, d]	N/A	N/A	N/A	N/A	N/A	N/A	N/A	27.9	26.9	27.9	26.2	23.4	21.6	19.8
Sedatives[d]	18.2	17.7	17.4	16.0	14.6	14.9	16.0	15.2	14.4	13.3	11.8	10.4	8.7	7.8
Barbiturates[d]	16.9	16.2	15.6	13.7	11.8	11.0	11.3	10.3	9.9	9.9	9.2	8.4	7.4	6.7
Methaqualone[d]	8.1	7.8	8.5	7.9	8.3	9.5	10.6	10.7	10.1	8.3	6.7	5.2	4.0	3.3
Tranquilizers[d]	17.0	16.8	18.0	17.0	16.3	15.2	14.7	14.0	13.3	12.4	11.9	10.9	10.9	9.4
Alcohol	90.4	91.9	92.5	93.1	93.0	93.2	92.6	92.8	92.6	92.6	92.2	91.3	92.2	92.0
Cigarettes	73.6	75.4	75.7	75.3	74.0	71.0	71.0	70.1	70.6	69.7	68.8	67.6	67.2	66.4

[a] Inhalants adjusted for underreporting of amyl and butyl nitrites. [b] Hallucinogens adjusted for underreporting of PCP. [c] Stimulants adjusted to exclude inappropriate reporting of nonprescription stimulants. [d] Only use not under a doctor's orders included.

Source: U.S. Department of Health and Human Services, National Institute on Drug Abuse, Monitoring the Future Study, 1989.

serve lighter sentences. It may be presumed that many return to the streets more quickly to resume their trade than would occur under normal criminal justice procedures.

But prosecutors defend plea-bargaining for the relief it offers in the nation's overcrowded prisons. Wade B. Houk, the Federal Bureau of Prisons' assistant director for administration, reported in testimony before Congress in 1988 that the 1980s had witnessed an "unprecedented increase of 85 percent" in the federal inmate population. Much of the increase is related to the drug trade: Houk testified that the percentage of prison inmates incarcerated for drug offenses rose from only a quarter of the total inmate population in 1981 to more than 40 percent by 1988.[7] Incarceration of drug offenders is especially costly. Prison sentences for drug offenders—more than five years, on average—are longer than for any other category of federal offender except for those charged with violent crimes.[8]

Economic and Social Costs

Rising crime and other problems associated with the drug trade are raising the cost of illicit drugs to the nation as a whole. In 1983, the latest year for which data are available, the United States spent about $60 billion in expenses for prison, law-enforcement, and other criminal justice services, for lost employment, and for treatment programs aimed at the buyers and sellers of illicit drugs.[9] With the spread of crack, that sum has undoubtedly risen significantly since 1983. In some areas, effects of the drug trade are straining local budgets as well. In Washington, D.C., for example, the thriving drug industry has forced the city government to increase spending for the prison system, the police department, and the courts.

But even the billions of dollars spent in direct ways to curtail the drug trade understate the economic effects of the trade on this country. They do not, for example, include the social costs involved in the growing numbers of children and youths who end up in the criminal justice system long before they have completed their education or training for legitimate employment. In Washington, D.C., 2,023 of the 5,127 children from nine to seventeen years of age who went before D.C. Superior Court in 1987 were charged with possession or sale of narcotics, more than twice the number registered the year before.[10] At the same time, children increasingly are victims of drug-related violence. Washington again provides an example. On average, one child or teenager was shot or stabbed each day in 1988, an unprecedented incidence of juvenile assaults that police attributed to turf battles among drug dealers.[11]

The arrival of crack and, in some cities, an upsurge in the use of PCP and other dangerous substances, has increased the number of addicted Americans and raised the death toll among drug users (Table 6-2). Health

Table 6-2 Population Estimates of Lifetime and Current Recreational Drug Use, 1988 (population in thousands)

	12-17 years (pop. 20,250)				18-25 years (pop. 29,688)				26+ years (pop. 148,409)				Total (pop. 198,347)			
	%	*Ever used*	%	*Current user*	%	*Ever used*	%	*Current user*	%	*Ever used*	%	*Current user*	%	*Ever used*	%	*Current user*
Marijuana & Hashish	17	3,516	6	1,296	56	16,741	16	4,594	31	45,491	4	5,727	33	65,748	6	11,616
Hallucinogens	3	704	1	168	14	4,093	2	569	7	9,810	°	°	7	14,607	°	°
Inhalants	9	1,774	2	410	12	3,707	2	514	4	5,781	°	°	6	11,262	1	1,223
Cocaine	3	683	1	225	20	5,858	5	1,323	10	14,631	1	1,375	11	21,171	2	2,923
Crack	1	188	°	°	3	1,000	1	249	°	°	°	°	1	2,483	°	484
Heroin	1	118	°	°	°	°	°	°	1	1,686	°	°	1	1,907	°	°
Stimulants	4	852	1	245	11	3,366	2	718	7	9,850	1	791	7	14,068	1	1,755
Sedatives	2	475	1	123	6	1,633	1	265	3	4,867	°	°	4	6,975	°	°
Tranquilizers	2	413	°	°	8	2,319	1	307	5	6,750	1	822	5	9,482	1	1,174
Analgesics	4	840	1	182	9	2,798	1	440	5	6,619	°	°	5	10,257	1	1,151
Alcohol	50	10,161	25	5,097	90	26,807	65	19,392	89	131,530	55	81,356	85	168,498	53	105,845
Cigarettes	42	8,564	12	2,389	75	22,251	35	10,447	80	118,191	30	44,284	75	149,005	29	57,121
Smokeless tobacco	15	3,021	4	722	24	6,971	6	1,855	13	19,475	3	4,497	15	29,467	4	7,073

Note: Ever used: used at least once in a person's lifetime. Current user: used at least once in the thirty days prior to the survey.
° Amounts of less than .5% are not listed.

Source: U.S. Department of Health and Human Services, National Institute on Drug Abuse, August 1989.

officials estimated in late 1987 that there are 5,000 new cocaine users each day, that 6,000 use the drug regularly, and that between 200,000 and a million Americans are compulsive users of the drug.[12] Crack and PCP take a heavy toll among young people. Across the country, the number of cocaine-related deaths has more than doubled since 1983, when crack first appeared.[13] Altogether, 4,138 people died of drug overdose in the nation's hospital emergency rooms in 1986, almost twice the number recorded in 1981, according to the NIDA's Drug Abuse Warning Network. Although drug-related emergency admissions remained stable at about 120,000 over the same period, the number of patients admitted for cocaine-related emergencies was more than 24,000 in 1986, five times the 1981 figure.[14] These figures seem likely to rise again with the appearance in 1989 of increasing amounts of high-purity heroin, which has long been a leading cause of death by overdose. Heroin addicts were until recently a fairly stable and older population. But an emerging tendency among crack smokers to mix crack and heroin—a combination known as "speedball"—may push the death toll much higher.

Even when drugs do not kill, many have adverse health effects on users. Heroin's addictive nature is well known, but only recently has it been established that crack cocaine is even more addictive than any of the opiates. Crack also frequently induces paranoia and aggressive behavior, an effect that may explain some of the violence that surrounds its sale and use. PCP also induces aggressive behavior and is even more dangerous in that respect than crack. The drug's powerful anesthetic effects make the user numb to pain, and narcotics agents tell of having to employ several men to restrain a single PCP user who is under the drug's influence.

But the pharmacological effects of some illicit drugs are only part of the health problem. Users who take their drugs by intravenous (IV) injection are at high risk of contracting viral diseases, the most serious of which is acquired immune deficiency syndrome (AIDS). Drug users who inject heroin, cocaine, or other substances frequently share needles. A user infected with the AIDS virus can easily transmit the disease to someone else who uses the same needle. Initially confined largely to homosexual men and recipients of tainted blood transfusions, AIDS has spread dramatically among IV drug users who are rapidly transmitting this fatal disease to their needle-sharing and sexual partners.

By 1988, IV drug users had become the second-largest group of AIDS victims, accounting for a third of the more than 32,000 cases reported that year. In some areas, such as New York City, where heroin use is high, as many as 70 percent of IV drug users are infected. About 400,000 of the 1.2 million IV drug users in the United States are women, and because the AIDS virus passes easily through the placenta, infected pregnant women are spreading the disease to their children as well. As many as 5 percent of mothers at some inner-city hospitals are transferring the virus to their newborn children. The Presidential Commission on the Human Immunodeficiency Virus Epidemic predicted in 1988 that AIDS would strike between 10,000 and 20,000 infants and children by 1991, largely because of IV drug use.[15]

The Centers for Disease Control (CDC) estimate that as of January 1988, 23 percent of all reported AIDS cases were IV drug users. The CDC also provides the following estimates of the percentage of IV drug users in major U.S. cities who test positive for the AIDS virus.

City	Percentage
New York	50-60
Newark	50
Boston	28
New Haven	26
Chicago	25
Baltimore	25
Philadelphia	19
San Francisco	16
Atlanta	10
Miami	5
Detroit	5
Denver	5
Los Angeles	4
Minneapolis	2
Dallas	2
San Antonio	2

Source: Centers for Disease Control, *AIDS Weekly Surveillance Report*, August 15, 1988.

The incidence of heroin abuse among the nation's poor has always been much higher than for the population as a whole. The same connection is increasingly apparent with crack. Recent statistics show that crack use is growing rapidly, especially among women. One study of drug abuse patterns in Florida found that women at greatest risk are single, unemployed mothers and pregnant teenagers.[16] While marijuana was the most frequently abused drug among females between nine and seventeen years of age, cocaine was by far the most heavily used drug among females eighteen and older. Drug experts who have tracked the rise in female cocaine addiction speculate that women who stop short of IV heroin abuse may perceive smoking crack as less dangerous. For whatever reason, crack use has risen rapidly among women, a trend that has been linked to the growing incidence of child abuse and neglect. Although no one knows the extent of crack addiction, the portion of women seeking treatment at one of New York City's drug treatment centers jumped from 20 percent to 32 percent between 1985 and 1988.[17]

The damaging effects of drug abuse are most keenly felt by minorities, chiefly blacks and Hispanics. The rise in drug abuse among minority women threatens the already precarious family structure in their communities. More than 70 percent of the poorest black families were headed by women in 1980, according to the Census Bureau. More recent statistics show that the number of black and Hispanic families with female heads of household is increasing. When the mainstay of the family abuses drugs, she has little hope of finding employment or of providing a decent life for her children. Worse, many children are born already addicted because cocaine and other drugs pass easily through the placenta into the fetus's bloodstream. The National Association for Perinatal Addiction Research and Education reported in August 1988 that at least 11 percent of women it surveyed in thirty-six hospitals around the country had used illicit drugs during pregnancy.

Growing crack abuse among women has made cocaine the most common illicit drug found in newborn babies. Infants exposed to cocaine during fetal development are more likely to die before birth or to be born prematurely. Those who survive are more likely to be smaller than normal and have physical deformities such as small heads and brains, as well as genital and urinary tract malformations. They are ten times more likely to die of sudden infant death syndrome, or crib death, than drug-free babies. Other drugs also pose risks to normal fetal development. Both heroin and methadone, the drug that is most often used to help addicts recover, produce withdrawal symptoms in newborn babies, such as extreme irritability, rigidity of the arms and legs, and tremors. Even marijuana, whose adverse effects in adult users is highly controversial, has been observed to cause tremors and exaggerated reflexes in newborns, as well as impaired language development in childhood.[18]

The effects of drug abuse by pregnant mothers on their surviving children are beginning to constitute a special problem for schools. In some cities where abuse is high, such as Los Angeles, school officials and teachers must devise special strategies to educate "drug babies" who have learning disabilities. Because these children were exposed to different types and amounts of drugs during their prenatal development, there is some debate over the best ways to educate them. In a move that has sparked controversy, a school district in Los Angeles, for example, has isolated them from the rest of the elementary school children.[19]

Notes

1. State of the Union address delivered January 15, 1988, before a joint session of Congress.
2. U.S. Department of Health and Human Services, National Institute on Drug Abuse, *National Household Survey on Drug Abuse: Population Estimates 1985*, 1987.
3. U.S. Department of Health and Human Services, National Institute on Drug Abuse, *National Household Survey on Drug Abuse: Population Estimates 1988*, 1989.
4. Mary G. Graham, *Controlling Drug Abuse and Crime: A Research Update*, NIJ Reports—Drugs and Crime, March/April 1987.
5. Christopher A. Innes, *Drug Use and Crime*, U.S. Department of Justice, Bureau of Justice Statistics Special Report, July 1988, 1.
6. "An Addict Confesses to 600 Burglaries," *New York Times*, October 20, 1988, B4.
7. Wade B. Houk testified June 1, 1988, before the House Government Operations Subcommittee on Government Information, Justice, and Agriculture.
8. U.S. Department of Justice, Bureau of Justice Statistics, *Drug Law Violators, 1980-86*, 1.
9. General Accounting Office, Special Report from the Comptroller General of the United States, *Controlling Drug Abuse: A Status Report*, 1988, 3.
10. Victoria Churchville, "Number of Children in Court Doubles," *Washington Post*, June 2, 1988, D1.
11. Rene Sanchez, "Growing Web of Violence Traps D.C. Youth," *Washington Post*, October 12, 1988, A1.
12. Deborah M. Barnes, "Drugs: Running the Numbers," *Science*, June 24, 1988, 1729-1731.
13. General Accounting Office, *Controlling Drug Abuse*, 9.
14. U.S. Department of Health and Human Services, National Institute on Drug Abuse, *1981 Annual Report: Data from the Drug Abuse Warning Network*, and *1986 Annual Report: Data from the Drug Abuse Warning Network*.
15. Presidential Commission on the Human Immunodeficiency Virus Epidemic, *Chairman's Draft Recommendations for the Final Report*, June 2, 1988, 144.
16. The Ad Hoc Coalition on National Alcohol and Drug Issues held a briefing for members of Congress and their staffs on September 7, 1988. The Coalition discussed the Drug Abuse Act of 1988 and the substance abuse problem in Florida.
17. Peter Kerr, "Addiction's Hidden Toll: Poor Families in Turmoil," *New York Times*, June 23, 1988, A1.
18. Robin Marantz Henig, "Making Mothers-to-Be Abstain," *Washington Post* (Health supplement), September 13, 1988, 8.
19. Allan Parachini, "'Drug Babies' and the Schools," *Los Angeles Times*, October 25, 1988, V1.

7 Supply-Side Attempts to Destroy the Drug Industry

The government has long tried to mitigate the high social costs of drug abuse by disrupting the multibillion dollar industry that fosters it. The appropriate methods are a subject of mounting controversy, but most agree that attempts to eliminate the business of illicit drugs must focus on disrupting the basic economic equation that motivates any industry, the law of supply and demand. Over the years, federal antidrug policy has included efforts to affect both sides of this equation. During the 1980s, however, the Reagan administration's antidrug policy strongly emphasized the supply side. Of the total increase in federal drug-enforcement funds from 1982 to 1986, about 90 percent went into the effort to cut supply, according to the General Accounting Office (GAO).[1] With the passage of the 1986 Anti-Drug Abuse Act (PL 99-570), which increased funding for the war on drugs from just over $2 billion in 1986 to almost $4 billion in 1988, the bias toward supply reduction remained.

The supply-side approach seeks to reduce the availability of drugs at each phase of the distribution network, from the fields and processing laboratories to the consumer. Since the beginning of the decade, the roles played by federal agencies have changed to include greater participation by the military and the intelligence community and an unprecedented degree of coordination among the agencies. Today the FBI conducts drug investigations in collaboration with DEA. Thirteen different task forces using personnel from various agencies have been set up around the country to penetrate high-level drug trafficking rings. The National Narcotics Border Interdiction System was established to coordinate the activities of those agencies in stopping drug imports.

U.S. Efforts to Disrupt Foreign Sources

Efforts to limit the supply of drugs have focused on every step of the production process, from the field to the border to the street. The Departments of State, Justice, and Defense are actively involved in international efforts to disrupt the flow of drugs before they reach the United States. U.S. participation in these efforts includes the loan of helicopters and other equipment, training, and the provision of intelligence by American military personnel under the terms of bilateral military assistance agreements with drug-producing nations.

In the late 1980s, the Reagan administration gave special emphasis to destroying the plants that produce illicit drugs. By eradicating coca bushes and heroin poppies, the administration reasoned, the supply of drugs entering the United States could be drastically curtailed. It also claimed that it would be less costly and risky to eliminate drugs "at the source" than at any other stage along the chain of distribution.

Congress agreed, and with the Anti-Drug Abuse Act of 1986 expanded the programs to limit the production of drugs in foreign countries. In fiscal 1987, the Bureau of International Narcotics Matters, an office of the State Department, received a record $118 million from Congress to expand its "narcotics eradication" program. That year, twenty-three countries were involved in U.S. efforts to destroy drug-producing plants, up from just two countries in 1981. The results have been mixed. Former assistant secretary of state Ann B. Wrobleski, who headed the program, told Congress in 1988 that cannabis cultivation in Jamaica, Belize, and Colombia had been "sharply reduced" as a result of the eradication program. Bolivia also participated by initiating a coca-bush eradication program in 1987. That year, according to Wrobleski, her agency succeeded in destroying 5,046 metric tons of coca leaf in Latin America, as well as 283 metric tons of opium and 17,585 tons of cannabis in its worldwide eradication program. "These figures represent four times the amount of opium that reaches the United States as heroin, three times the amount of marijuana consumed in the United States and one-seventh the amount of coca leaf required for conversion into the cocaine consumed by American users," she wrote in answer to criticism of the eradication effort.[2]

Eradication programs are used to destroy marijuana and poppy plants, so-called narcotics crops, as well as coca. The biggest eradication program run by the United States is in Mexico, which in 1988 eradicated more than 12,000 acres of marijuana and opium poppy fields in the ten states along the Pacific coast.

But U.S.-sponsored eradication efforts have not been welcomed by all drug-producing countries. Where cultivation of drug crops enjoys a long tradition and has become the mainstay of large peasant populations, the eradication efforts are strongly resented as acts of Yankee imperialism. The use of herbicides has been especially controversial. Many countries collaborate with the United States by sending personnel into the fields to manually pull up and burn cannabis, coca, or poppy plants. But only a handful—Mexico, Belize, Panama, Colombia, Jamaica, Pakistan, and Burma, as of 1989—accept U.S. aid to use herbicides as a means of destroying illicit crops.

As concern over the spread of crack use has mounted, crop eradication efforts have focused on the Andean coca fields. With U.S. assistance, in 1988 local workers used power trimmers to destroy more than 13,000 acres of coca in the region. Eradication programs aimed at the cocaine industry, however, are too costly and slow to keep up with the coca growers, who are able to move quickly from targeted areas to areas not previously used for coca cultivation, often from one country to another. In addition, coca eradication is dangerous. Because drug agents have been killed in the fields as they attempted to manually destroy coca crops, in the spring of 1988 the State Department called for what Wrobleski termed "a chemical solution to widespread coca cultivation in the Andes." [3]

Although aerial spraying of coca fields with herbicides reduces the risks to personnel, it does pose hazards to the environment and to people who live near the sprayed areas. Tebuthiuron, or Spike 20P, the chemical that in early testing has proved most effective in killing the coca plant, is a highly toxic chemical that kills trees and shrubs when it comes into contact with the plants' root systems. Dropped in pellet form from helicopters, the chemical could also fall on adjoining areas, destroying harmless vegetation and thus worsening the growing problem of erosion in the mountainous coca-growing region. Once it dissolves on the ground, Spike can remain active for several years and could destroy vegetation far from the target areas as it is carried off by streams and rivers. The chemical may also kill fish and harm other animals and humans who come into contact with it. Citing these environmental dangers, as well as the risk of reprisals against company representatives in the countries where it would be used, Eli Lilly & Co. announced in May 1988 that it would not participate in the program. The Indianapolis-based company is the sole U.S. manufacturer of Spike, the herbicide chosen for use on coca in Peru. The State Department claims the chemical would cause less damage than the slash-and-burn techniques used in coca cultivation and the runoff of dangerous chemicals such as acetone and sulfuric acid that are used in the cocaine processing labs. But the governments of coca-growing countries remain skeptical. Bolivia has rejected aerial spraying in favor of the program of manual eradication it introduced in 1987. For his part, Peruvian president Alan Garcia has expressed support for aerial spraying of coca fields, pending further tests of Spike's environmental effects.

Eradication schemes have envisioned crop substitution as an incentive for peasant farmers who currently cultivate drug-producing plants. In return for his conditional support of aerial spraying, in fact, Garcia asks for greater U.S. support of alternative sources of income for the thousands of peasants who depend on coca cultivation for their livelihood. But crop substitution is a daunting undertaking, as Rensselaer Lee, an expert on the South American drug trade, illustrates. A Bolivian coca farmer can earn as much as $2,500 per hectare a year, more than four times what he can net from growing oranges or avocados, the next most profitable crops. The United States now pays the equivalent of $2,000 per hectare of eradicated coca in Bolivia. But, Lee says, the cost of replacing coca with an alternative crop is closer to $7,000 per hectare. Because 50,000-70,000 hectares are now used for growing coca in Bolivia, Lee estimates, it would take $350 million to $490 million to pay for total eradication of coca and substitution with legal crops in that country alone.[4]

Destruction of Processing Labs

An older approach to reducing the supply of drugs is the disruption of the drug-refining process. Cocaine laboratories in Bolivia were the target of a massive U.S. effort in the summer of 1986. In an operation code-named Operation Blast Furnace, units of the U.S. Army destroyed labs in the Bolivian forest, after which the State Department lent the Bolivian Air Force six military helicopters to continue the operation alone. The effort succeeded in disrupting cocaine production in that country for about three months.

As the U.S. further emphasized the supply side of the drug trade, these efforts have received greater support. In 1987 DEA launched Operation Snowcap, a three-year Latin American antidrug campaign involving U.S. Army Special Forces, the U.S. Border Patrol, and local police forces. The program focuses on destroying coca-processing laboratories, clandestine landing strips, and traffickers' operations in the coca-producing areas. U.S. military personnel provide training in jungle operations, navigation, the use of weapons, and survival skills to some 150 DEA agents assigned to Latin American countries to assist local police forces.

"Search-and-destroy" missions against jungle processing laboratories expose enforcement agents to less danger than manually eradicating plants in the ground. But even surgical strikes are taking their toll, especially in Peru's Upper Huallaga Valley. As Shining Path and the Tupac Amaru Revolutionary Movement increased their control over the valley, DEA agents assigned to assist in Operation Snowcap came under fire. They were forced to abandon their main operating base in the town of Tingo Maria when it was attacked and taken over by guerrilla forces in March 1989.

But even when limited to training teams and military advisers that act only behind the scenes, the involvement of U.S. forces in overseas drug enforcement carries political risks that few governments are willing to accept. More fundamentally, efforts to destroy coca labs face the same problems as crop eradication. Even if a lab is destroyed, processors can easily move their rudimentary facilities to other sites, well hidden under the jungle canopy.

The United States receives the cooperation of many countries in its efforts to cut off drugs at the source. In 1988 the U.S.-led International Drug Enforcement Conference, a coalition of twenty nations of the Western Hemisphere, collaborated with Nigeria and nine European countries in destroying coca-processing labs and airstrips in Central and South America. Attorney General Richard Thornburgh said the coalition's four-week crackdown provided a model for future collaboration in the war on drugs. "Each of the nations of the Americas has been pursuing the war on drugs in a more or less unilateral or bilateral fashion," he said. "There has been, to be sure, sharing of data and isolated cases of close cooperation, but never before has there been such systematic and comprehensive cooperation." [5]

Extradition Treaties

Where local governments have been left to run antidrug programs with U.S. financial assistance alone, the United States has beefed up its local role by invoking bilateral extradition treaties. Their purpose is to bring important figures in the drug trade to trial in the United States, where they would face a greater likelihood of conviction as well as stiffer sentences. But extradition is widely unpopular in drug-producing countries. In many cases, drug crops are the most profitable sources of income for impoverished peasants, who look on the drug lords as the guarantors of their survival. In 1988, for example, the extradition to the United States of Juan Ramon Matta Ballesteros from Honduras sparked anti-American riots in the streets of Tegucigalpa. Fearing such political unrest, many governments in drug-producing countries have resisted U.S. pressure to extradite traffickers. In Colombia the Supreme Court in 1987 struck down implementing legislation for a bilateral extradition treaty with the United States. It took the drug lords' assassination of a popular presidential candidate in 1989 to reverse the public's opposition to the treaty and prepare the way for the extradition of several cocaine traffickers.

The potential for extradition as a useful deterrent to high-level drug dealers was enhanced in December 1988, when forty-three members of the United Nations signed an international convention against drug trafficking and drug abuse. The agreement, which was nearly three years in the making, contained an unprecedented provision granting all signatories the right to extradite suspected drug traffickers and to confiscate their assets. Because it is multilateral, the agreement may make it easier for Latin American signatories to avert the domestic resentment of U.S. intervention that has hampered U.S. antidrug efforts.

Country Certification Process

The Anti-Drug Abuse Act of 1986 implemented a carrot-and-stick approach to reducing the overseas supply of drugs to this country, aimed as much toward the countries where the illicit drug industry thrives as toward the entrepreneurs themselves. It requires the president to certify whether major drug-producing and drug-transit countries have "cooperated fully" with the United States or acted on their own initiative to prevent drug production and trafficking. The law also requires the president to identify major illicit drug producing or drug transit countries, a label President Reagan attached to twenty-four nations in February 1987.[6] The incentive for foreign governments to cooperate is the provision of U.S. personnel and equipment, including helicopters and herbicides, to the recipient country's antidrug campaign. A country's failure to cooperate in the eradication effort would result in trade sanctions and the loss of American aid.

The law also requires the president to sanction countries unless he reports to Congress each year that they are currently cooperating with U.S. narcotics control efforts, or that applying sanctions would harm U.S. vital national interests. Countries that do not receive the president's certification receive only half the foreign aid that they were due to receive that year. At the beginning of fiscal 1988, about $1.5 billion in U.S. assistance were suspended as a result of the certification proceedings. The law also requires the United States to vote against extending loans to these countries by such multilateral institutions as the World Bank. The president may, at his discretion, also impose trade sanctions and suspend commercial airline service to these countries. The president's decisions in the certification process can be overturned by a joint resolution of Congress. Wrobleski told Congress that the threat of withheld funds has paid off. "I think Bolivia's decision to enter into an eradication agreement, Panama's decision to pass antinarcotics legislation that permitted money laundering investigations, Pakistan's decision to spray opium poppy, and numerous other decisions reflected a heightened awareness on the part of governments in every region that denial of certification and lost benefits were very real possibilities," she told a congressional panel in June 1988.[7]

But, as Wrobleski went on to acknowledge, the certification process is not free of controversy. Although the law calls for denial of aid to countries that do not cooperate fully with U.S. antinarcotics efforts, circumstances vary widely among drug-producing nations. Colombia's chaotic internal conditions caused by the cocaine barons make that country's government far less capable of cooperating with eradication and other enforcement efforts than, say, Mexico. Not surprisingly, the State Department and members of Congress have differed over what constitutes cooperation. The controversy flared in 1988, when members of Congress disputed the president's determinations of certification for several countries involved in the illicit drug trade. The Senate voted to disapprove the certification of Mexico, and the whole Congress voted against the certification of the Bahamas, Bolivia, Paraguay, and Peru.

The controversy has been most heated over Mexico. Critics in the United States say the Mexican government has not cooperated fully with U.S. efforts, and the Mexican government has been harshly criticized for failing to bring to trial the murderers of Enrique Camarena Salazar, the DEA agent killed while investigating a Mexican drug ring. Mexico attracted further condemnation by refusing to include in a recent bilateral agreement provisions that would allow for joint border patrols or cross-border "hot pursuit" of drug suspects by U.S. law-enforcement officials. Before taking office in 1988, President Carlos Salinas de Gortari promised to introduce an aggressive crackdown against his country's traffickers. But since then, some top Mexican law-enforcement officials have been accused of active involvement in some of the country's biggest drug trafficking operations. In February, just as the U.S. Senate was preparing to issue its annual list of countries found to have cooperated with U.S. drug-enforcement efforts, the chief of Mexico City's police intelligence unit, Miguel Nazar Haro, abruptly resigned. Nazar Haro, currently wanted by the United States for skipping bail on a charge of helping direct a car-theft ring in San Diego, has been linked in testimony to narcotics trafficking organizations as well.

Cost Effectiveness of Overseas Supply-Side Efforts

Quite apart from the controversy over which countries merit exemption from U.S. economic sanctions, the federal government's efforts to stanch the flow of drugs by eliminating them at the source have failed. As Rensselaer Lee points out, annual expenditures of $40-$50 million for U.S.-sponsored supply-side programs in the Andean cocaine-producing countries are hardly an obstacle to that $3-$4 billion a year industry. But spending more money is not the answer, he says. In his view, the very nature of the illicit drug trade in developing countries poses huge obstacles to a supply-side solution. First, governments often have no control over the drug-producing areas. Lee points to Peru's Upper Huallaga Valley, where Colombian cocaine traders have more influence than the Peruvian government. The same is true in other regions active in the production of other drugs. The heroin trade flourishes in areas of Burma, Afghanistan, and Pakistan where national governments have lost effective control.

Another obstacle to supply-side solutions is corruption. In countries where government officials, judges, and police agents are bribed by drug entrepreneurs, there can be no effective law enforcement. Lee cites the example of Bolivian coca paste traffickers, who routinely pay police $7,000-$8,000 a day not to interfere with shipments of paste from the Chapare. In Colombia cartel leaders live virtually free of harassment in their home territories around Medellin and Cali. Even when arrested, they often bribe their way out of prison. Governments of poor nations, many of which owe large debts to foreign banks, are ill-equipped to counter the lure of large bribes. And of course, in some countries such as Noriega's Panama, leading government officials themselves are the major benefactors of the drug trade.

Further obstacles to supply-side solutions to America's drug problem are linked to the lack of popular support of enforcement efforts in the supplier nations. In some countries, such as Bolivia and Peru, there is a long tradition of coca use and little concern about its dangers when refined into the more potent forms that are sold on the streets of North America. This perception may be changing slowly as local populations in producer countries begin to be exposed to refined products. In addition, the illicit drug industry is usually the best employer in producer countries, even when it means only subsistence earnings for rural growers of poppy, cannabis, or coca. As in other threatened industries, the employees are vehemently opposed to seeing their source of livelihood closed down. Offers of alternative employment, such as rural development programs calling for crop substitution or industrial development, are rarely appealing. For one thing, they are unlikely to provide as high earnings as the drug trade, at least in the short term. Even more importantly, drug traffickers in some countries have not hesitated to kill peasant farmers who cooperate in crop substitution programs.

A final obstacle to U.S. efforts to cut the supply of drugs is political. Developing countries have watched the industrial giant to the north prosper as they have grown more slowly and, in recent years, stagnated under the load of heavy foreign debt. Popular sympathy often is stronger for local drug barons than for the consumers of their trade on America's streets.

Such structural barriers to effective supply-side antidrug policy are, in Lee's opinion, virtually insurmountable. Even where local governments cooperate fully with U.S.-sponsored programs, he concludes, "the core structure of the cocaine industry—its organization, leadership, and refining and marketing infrastructure—remains more or less intact. And the industry's agricultural base continues to expand; for every hectare of coca eradicated, two or three hectares are planted elsewhere."[8]

Interdiction at the Border

Even while programs to cut off drugs at the source are expanded, the real war on drugs is being conducted closer to home. Judging from the funding and manpower involved, the federal government has intensified its supply-side effort to destroy the drug trade at the U.S. border.

These so-called interdiction efforts, traditionally the job of the customs service and the coast guard, have increasingly involved the regular military as well. The use of the armed forces for civilian law enforcement is prohibited by the 1878 Posse Comitatus Act. But in 1981, during

Reagan's first year in office, Congress amended the law to allow police access to military intelligence information. The military now pass on information about drug-trafficking activities observed during offshore military operations to the police in the border areas where the drugs appear to be headed. While the functions of the police and the military are still separated by law, there are provisions for limited cooperation between the two.[9]

The 1986 Anti-Drug Abuse Act further expanded the military's role in drug enforcement by providing for the loan of helicopters, radar, and other equipment to law-enforcement agencies. Accordingly, the Defense Department has furnished some $360 million worth of mobile radar and ground sensor equipment for use in detecting smuggling activities and has trained police officers in their use.

The distinction between civilian law-enforcement agencies and the armed forces continues to fade. In 1987 the Reagan administration declared drug smuggling over the borders a "national security threat to the United States" and issued a "declaration of war on drugs," language that implied a greater role for the armed forces in interdiction.[10] That same year, the navy participated with the coast guard in Operation Hat Trick, a campaign that also involved federal, state, and local police units in apprehending drug smugglers at the border. The military services also provided more than 17,000 hours of aerial surveillance to help detect smugglers before they reached the border. In 1988 the military clocked more than 28,000 hours in aerial support.

In addition, the Pentagon provided new navy and air force "over-the-horizon" radar systems to help the customs service and the coast guard detect drug shipments before they reached the border, deployed an army helicopter detachment in the Bahamas to transport local police on drug raids, and augmented its radar network in the Caribbean.

But some policy makers believed the new role of the military in drug interdiction did not go far enough. In early 1988 a heated debate erupted between city officials across the United States (including Mayor Edward Koch of New York City), other policy makers concerned about the impact of drugs on society, and military spokesmen who said that drug interdiction was a police concern. Sen. Sam Nunn, D-Ga., chairman of the Senate Armed Services Committee, joined former defense secretary Caspar Weinberger and then-secretary Frank Carlucci in arguing that further involvement of the armed services in drug interdiction along the borders would distract them from their traditional defense mission and impair the country's military readiness.

The controversy peaked in mid-1988, when Congress considered measures that called for more direct military involvement in the war on drugs, including proposals to allow the military to make drug arrests. Although these proposals were later dropped from the fiscal 1989 defense authorization bill, Congress earmarked $308 million for an expanded role of the armed services in interdiction efforts. It also designated the Defense Department as the lead agency for coordinating air and sea surveillance of illegal drug traffic over U.S. borders. In February 1989 the Pentagon assigned responsibility for the new surveillance to the coast guard, setting up task forces for the Atlantic and Pacific coasts under the charge of two coast guard admirals.

The Pentagon also assigned the National Guard a greater role in antidrug activities. In September 1987 the National Guard participated in a joint interdiction program with the customs service along the Arizona-Mexico border. But Operation Autumn Harvest, as the program was called, resulted in no drug interdictions and was criticized in a report by the General Accounting Office, which found that "Operation Autumn Harvest was not adequately coordinated and that Customs was not sufficiently involved in the planning."[11]

The GAO report reflects the confusion that has surrounded the new government policy toward drug interdiction. As support grows for a greater military role in stopping drugs at the border, the agencies traditionally responsible for monitoring cross-border traffic, chiefly customs, are left without a clear mandate. The 1986 Anti-Drug Abuse Act charged customs with the job of coordinating the interdiction operations carried out by five federal agencies. But just two years later, the Pentagon's designation as lead agency in interdiction activities diminished the role of customs and incited interagency rivalry.[12]

More important, the emphasis on interdiction at the borders is not meeting expectations. In fiscal 1988 interdiction operations accounted for more than $1 billion in federal drug-enforcement expenditures, about a fourth of the enforcement budget and by far the biggest single program. But despite the new funding, and increased interdiction efforts since 1981, Peter Reuter of Rand finds that cocaine imports have increased. Even more significantly, increased interdiction did not raise cocaine prices as expected. Instead, prices fell, from about $600,000 a kilo for one-gram packets at retail in 1981, to $250,000 in 1987.[13]

Reuter offers what he calls a "speculative but entirely plausible" explanation for this apparent defiance of economic logic.

> This is the notion that as dealers get experienced they get better at controlling their risks. As dealers get experienced, the retail price of drugs will tend to go down because each of them now has lower costs. This will build over time, even with intensified interdiction, which tends to catch the less experienced dealers. So even if you are catching more dealers, the number of experienced dealers keeps going up as the market expands. That means that the supply curve keeps shifting up as the price goes down.

Reuter's idea that the cocaine boom in the United States is building the ranks of experienced smugglers is supported by the evidence. Despite the joint efforts of the coast guard and the customs service to detect airborne drug runners along the southern border with the latest in the Pentagon's radar detection equipment, only about 12 percent of smugglers' planes are being captured. To have an effect on price, two to three times that number must be seized.[14]

Supply-Side Measures against the Domestic Drug Industry

Eradication of drugs at the source, destruction of processing labs, and interdiction at the border have not succeeded in stopping the flow of illegal drugs into the United States. But the supply-side approach to drug suppression does not stop at the border. At home as well, federal efforts to solve the drug problem have focused on availability.

One segment of the illegal drug industry, the marijuana trade, is a candidate for one of the solutions practiced outside the United States, eradication. Because it is the only major plant-derived illegal substance cultivated domestically, the finished marijuana product does not depend on imported ingredients. Unlike cocaine, whose availability has not been adversely affected by stepped-up eradication and interdiction campaigns of recent years, marijuana's bulk and telltale aroma make it more sensitive to efforts to seal the border against its importation. Because of the drug's relatively low market price and the increased risk of interdiction at the border, the profitability of marijuana trafficking for foreign suppliers has diminished, explaining in large part the boom in marijuana production in the United States during the late 1980s.

The National Narcotics Intelligence Consumers Committee estimates that fully a quarter of the marijuana sold on the U.S. market in 1987 was domestically produced, up from only 18 percent one year earlier. Marijuana greenhouses have been seized in every state.

The federal government's answer to the booming business of marijuana cultivation has been the same as its response to cocaine and heroin growers overseas, an emphasis on eliminating the drug at the source. Instead of the State Department, which runs overseas eradication efforts, DEA is the agency in charge of domestic marijuana eradication, providing support to state and local agencies through its "domestic cannabis eradication/suppression program." First introduced in 1979 in Hawaii and California, the program has been implemented in all fifty states at one time or another. In much the same way it does to foreign governments seeking to combat drug production, DEA's main function in U.S.

eradication efforts is to provide funds, training, and equipment such as aircraft to state and local agencies, which then carry out the marijuana eradication themselves. DEA spent nearly $4 million on cannabis eradication in 1987.

The most widely publicized state and local pot eradication program is California's Campaign Against Marijuana Planting (CAMP). CAMP operations, set up in 1983, have involved county sheriff departments as well as other state and federal agencies and have resulted in numerous arrests and the eradication of hundreds of thousands of sinsemilla plants. But the program has been criticized for its high cost; it has been estimated that while the national average cost of eradicating a single marijuana plant was just $1.33 in 1984, CAMP spent $9.20 to destroy each plant.[15]

A more basic criticism of CAMP is the program's ineffectiveness in deterring marijuana cultivation outside its area of operations. According to the National Drug Enforcement Policy Board, "CAMP has displaced some of the problem to Oregon. The remaining commercial growers tend to view CAMP as a cost of doing business and take a variety of measures to minimize associated costs. Production has increased and product availability appears to have remained unchanged."[16] Judging from the California experience, aggressive eradication of drugs at the source presents the same shortcomings in the United States as it does in Latin America. Just as coca growers in the Andes have moved to areas that are not under heavy surveillance, American marijuana cultivators are leaving California to plant in areas where enforcement is less stringent. By choosing remote National Forest System lands for marijuana cultivation, U.S. growers face fewer risks of asset seizure if apprehended. Federal eradication efforts have focused on these lands in recent years, and Forest Service law-enforcement officers were authorized by the 1986 Anti-Drug Abuse Act to make drug arrests. The 1986 drug law also provided more money for the agency's antidrug activities, about $3 million in fiscal 1988. As it does for state and local enforcement agencies, DEA provides training and technical assistance to the Forest Service for its eradication program. William L. Rice, the Forest Service's deputy chief for administration, estimates that the agency now destroys about 40 percent of the entire cannabis crop grown in its jurisdiction.

But marijuana eradication has not seriously disrupted the domestic pot market. The congressional Committee on Government Operations report on marijuana production concluded that "although eradication and investigative activities have forced some growers to modify their cultivation techniques, they have failed to reduce the general availability of domestic marijuana."[17] The recent rise in street prices for the drug is due more to changes in the product's quality than to reduced availability. Domestic pot growers are producing more of the highly concentrated, more expensive sinsemilla, pushing up the average retail price of marijuana sold on the U.S. market.

State and Local Enforcement

With the exception of marijuana eradication, the main goal of domestic drug-enforcement policy has been to disrupt the distribution of the finished product to consumers. Federal legislation has directed funds to the state and local levels where authorities might decide how best to use them according to local market conditions. The 1986 Anti-Drug Abuse Act, for example, earmarked $225 million of its total $1.7 billion for local drug enforcement. It called on the Justice Department's Bureau of Justice Assistance to expedite the transfer of the funds to state and local narcotics control programs. The states set up drug policy boards to formulate a drug strategy and to coordinate the activities of the federal, state, and local agencies.

Plans to implement the law ran into problems immediately. For one thing, the level of federal funding was too low to provide significant help to all the local jurisdictions needing it. According to Bureau of Justice Assistance Director Charles P. Smith, "Forty-seven of the fifty-six states and territories which receive funds under the Anti-Drug Abuse Act received awards of less than $5 million in fiscal 1987. Using a jurisdiction by jurisdiction allocation, the local funds in most states would be reduced to a level of insignificance."[18]

States in which the illegal drug trade is flourishing have responded with tougher laws of their own. In California, where much of the cocaine business is linked to Los Angeles-based gangs, the state legislature passed a $9.45 million narcotics program in 1988. About a third of the funds were earmarked for the creation of an Organized Crime Strike Force whose main targets are the Bloods and Crips, the biggest umbrella gang organizations in Los Angeles.

In January 1989, New York governor Mario M. Cuomo unveiled a comprehensive new antidrug program to combat "the single most ominous phenomenon of our times." The eighteen-point program, which he called New York's top priority for 1989, includes a proposal to allow enforcement agents to seize property that is linked to the illegal drug business. This goes beyond an existing state law allowing agents to seize property bought with the proceeds of drug sales and would bring the state statutes into line with federal law, which allows for the confiscation of properties where such transactions take place, including shooting galleries, crack houses, and places where drugs are cooked or otherwise prepared for sale. To pay for the antidrug program in financially strapped New York, Cuomo proposed raising state taxes on alcoholic beverages and cigarettes.

Because the most frequent victims of the drug trade are children and juveniles, many jurisdictions have instituted "drug-free zones" around schools. First introduced in New Jersey, the zones are well defined areas in the vicinity of school grounds in which the penalties for selling drugs are especially severe. The laws typically call for prison terms without parole for dealers operating within 1,000 feet of school property.

One of the more pervasive legislative changes that states across the country have adopted to slow the spread of illegal drugs is stiffer mandatory sentencing of those convicted of drug dealing. In Maryland, for example, where current law imposes no minimum jail sentence for first-time offenders, a bill introduced in early 1989 would mandate a minimum five-year sentence for anyone convicted of producing or selling illegal drugs. Stiffer sentencing requirements, however, are translating into heavy prison overcrowding. Already a problem before the cocaine boom of the 1980s, overcrowding in some states has overwhelmed the prison system's ability to cope. In New York the number of drug felons in prison is five times higher than at the beginning of the decade. The same phenomenon is evident in federal prisons, where almost half the inmates are drug offenders and facilities house 58 percent more convicts than they were designed to hold. The ironic upshot of this trend is that even as stiffer sentencing laws are passed, convicted drug dealers are serving less of their time. To ease overcrowding, states are forced to release prisoners earlier.[19]

Not all states with heavy illegal drug activity have beefed up local enforcement. Virginia, with rapidly spreading cocaine sales in its Washington, D.C., suburbs and elsewhere, has rejected some fifty drug enforcement proposals, including the death penalty for dealers who sell dangerous substances to youths under sixteen, primarily on the grounds that they violate the rights of the accused.[20]

The federal statute with perhaps the greatest influence on state and local efforts to disrupt the illegal drug trade is the 1984 Comprehensive Crime Control Act. It provides for the "equitable sharing" of the proceeds gained from selling seized assets of drug dealers. Before it was passed, the federal government kept all the money made from dealers' property, including expensive cars, boats, mansions, bank accounts, and other valuables that have become the hallmark of successful drug dealers in the 1980s. Such asset seizures yielded the government more than $1 billion in 1987, up from $100 million in 1981. Congress changed the law to give state and local enforcement agencies part of the proceeds as an incentive to cooperate in federal drug-enforcement activities.[21] Since then, some local jurisdictions have benefited greatly: The Los Angeles Police Department, for example, was expected to receive about half the $88 million in cash it seized from drug dealers during the first four years of the equitable sharing arrangement.[22] Critics of the law, however, say that because assets are often seized before the suspects are convicted or even charged for selling drugs, it may violate the constitutional right of due process.

As the war on drugs continues to focus on suppressing the supply of illegal substances, similar concerns are being expressed about other enforcement practices. Federal law allows agents to seize and seal off buildings where dealers are in business, even if the action means evicting tenants not involved in the illegal trade. In New York City dozens of innocent residents were evicted from nearly 100 buildings in 1988. Mayor Ed Koch, who supports the federal seizures themselves, has called for a change to allow the city to continue to operate the buildings so that innocent tenants might continue to live in them.[23]

Despite concerns about due process and about the nation's growing homeless population, eviction has been embraced as a further deterrent to drug dealers from Los Angeles to Annapolis, Maryland. Los Angeles mayor Tom Bradley and Police Chief Daryl Gates have proposed a local ordinance that would require landlords to evict suspects arrested for dealing drugs in a rented house or apartment. And some cities are going beyond simple eviction: In 1988 the city government of Tampa, Florida, used money it seized in drug assets to finance the bulldozing of several crack houses in the city. In February 1989 New York City demolished a Brooklyn tenement that had been a center of cocaine and crack distribution. By destroying the building, which also served as a shooting gallery, city officials hoped to break up the drug-based micro-economy that it housed.

Property seizures, evictions, and building demolitions are all an offshoot of many local governments' decisions to take their efforts in the war on drugs to the streets, where the final transactions are made. Cities across the nation have hired more police, increased their overtime assignments, and devised new police strategies in an effort to disrupt the drug business. After the February 1988 slaying of Edward Byrne, a New York City rookie police officer who was guarding a drug-case witness's house in Brooklyn, the city created a new Tactical Narcotics Team (TNT). The team is known for its "buy and bust" sequence: Undercover officers buy drugs from street dealers, then "ghost" officers observing the transaction alert a team of uniformed police who make the arrest and try to obtain information about the seller's supplier higher up in the chain of distribution. Initially concentrated in Brooklyn, TNT units have since moved their operations to other areas of the city as well.

The Los Angeles approach to drug enforcement has become identified with "the Hammer," the police department's highly visible and controversial tactic in which hundreds of uniformed police officers surround neighborhoods where drugs are sold and make sweeping arrests. Police Chief Daryl Gates adopted the policy in February 1988 "to make life miserable" for drug dealers, especially those connected to the violent gang confederations. As the gangs have spread their distribution networks beyond the Los Angeles area, the cities they have targeted are also adopting defensive tactics. Seattle, for example, has called on federal agents to help local police identify and interrogate suspected gang members at the city's airports and bus and rail stations before they reach the streets and establish a drug franchise. Agents rely on "dealer profiles," descriptions provided by informants, to identify suspected dealers.[24] Seattle's strategy was being studied by other West Coast and Midwestern cities as a promising way of preventing the Los Angeles-based distributors from taking root. But other jurisdictions have rejected the dealer profile as an infringement on the rights of suspects against unreasonable seizure. The Virginia Court of Appeals, for example, ruled in May 1988 that police could not stop vehicles to search for drugs solely on the basis of the occupants' alleged resemblance to dealer profiles. While the Supreme Court did not directly address the issue of dealer profiles, it lent indirect support to their legitimacy with an April 1989 ruling that drug enforcement agents may detain any traveler whose behavior arouses "reasonable suspicion" of involvement in drug sales.

The Fight against Drugs in Washington, D.C.—An Uphill Battle

No city illustrates the difficulty of uprooting the business of illegal drugs as keenly as Washington, D.C. The city's role as the center of the nation's political life underlines the problem all the more strongly. Some of the city's most active open-air drug markets bustle with activity just a few blocks from the White House and Congress. "Washington has more drugs per square foot than anywhere in the nation," explains Sgt. Pat Moyer of the U.S. Park Police. "Drugs can be bought at seven in the morning in certain areas, and sales are made in broad daylight." The tragic corollary to Washington's dominant role in the drug trade is its recent ascent to the rank of the nation's number one murder capital as well. In 1988 there were 372 homicides in the city, most of which were drug related.

Like Los Angeles, New York City, and other urban centers of the illegal drug trade, Washington has adopted aggressive supply-side strategies to do its part in the war on drugs. In August 1986 the city adopted Operation Clean Sweep, a drug-enforcement program manned primarily by full-time police officers assigned to overtime duty and aimed at disrupting retail distribution networks rather than increasing arrests. By March 1989 the program had netted 46,000 arrests on drug-related charges at a cost of $6 million in overtime pay to participating officers, according to former police chief Maurice T. Turner, Jr. With the continuing upward spiral in drug-related violence, the District government in early 1989 declared a crime emergency: Hundreds of police officers were reassigned from administrative posts to the streets to heighten the visibility of the city's 3,800-member police force. The city council also passed tougher sentences for crimes involving drugs and firearms, including a minimum five-year sentence for felons who use real or imitation firearms while committing a crime. It later raised mandatory minimum sentences for convicted drug dealers and crack house operators by as much as six times.

But critics saw the latest measures as futile at best. The District has had mandatory sentences for drug dealers on the books since 1981. But the criminal justice system simply cannot handle the higher number of accused felons that would be brought before it under the sentencing measure. And the prison system, already overloaded, could not begin to absorb the additional inmates. As in other jurisdictions, plea-bargaining has become the solution for the vast majority of drug-related cases.

Frustration with the inability of the police and the criminal justice and prison systems to curtail the drug trade in Washington has led to proposals to call in the National Guard to lend a hand. Some say only a military presence has the firepower to drive the armed drug dealers from the streets. Others, including Mayor Marion Barry, say the National Guard would merely escalate tensions that already run high because of the rising homicide rate.

In late 1988 the mayor himself was linked to a suspected cocaine dealer. Although he repeatedly denied that he had ever taken drugs or been involved with the illegal drug trade, the scandal severely eroded the mayor's credibility as the city's leader in the fight against drugs.

Community Efforts to Thwart the Business of Illegal Drugs

As federal, state, and local law-enforcement agencies prove incapable of disrupting the illegal drug supply, communities across the country are taking the matter into their own hands. Local school boards are adopting new guidelines to prevent the drug business from entering school grounds. These range from stricter punishment of students caught pushing drugs, including suspension and expulsion, to patrols of the hallways. Some systems, including the Dade County public schools in Miami, Florida, ban paging beepers. The Fairfax County school system in northern Virginia, the largest suburban system in the Washington, D.C., metropolitan area, announced in early 1989 that it would monitor high schools with portable metal detectors and drug-sniffing dogs to find weapons and drugs brought onto school property.

But the most visible sign of citizen frustration is the appearance in communities across the nation of citizens' groups taking to the streets to drive dealers out of their neighborhoods. Some of these, such as the Neighborhood Watch groups that have formed throughout the United States since the mid-1970s, work in conjunction with local police. Volunteers armed with no more than citizens' band radios take turns patrolling neighborhood streets and reporting suspicious activity to the police. Police support the effort because it relieves understaffed departments of routine patrolling activities and allows officers to concentrate on crisis points.

The arrival of crack has prompted still more drastic action. The retail end of the crack trade quickly transforms entire neighborhoods. Because the effects of a crack high are short-lived, addicts tend to frequent the retail outlets for long periods of time and search the area for money for the next fix. Homes are burgled, pedestrians are robbed, and female addicts prostitute themselves. Turf wars among competing dealers turn neighborhoods into war zones, making it unsafe for residents to leave their homes at any hour. In these neighborhoods, typically working-class areas, some residents have reacted with violence to the crack trade. In Miami and Detroit, suspicious fires in buildings where drugs are sold suggest that citizens are resorting to arson in an effort to save their neighborhoods. In Detroit, two local residents confessed to setting fire to a neighborhood crack house in November 1987 after police failed to roust the dealers. Tried for arson, the two were acquitted of all charges, a sign of growing public sympathy for citizen action against drug dealers, even when such action amounts to vigilantism.

Most communities have turned to less drastic, but no less controversial, action by forming groups of volunteers to keep the drug trade away. Some of these groups are set up to meet purely local needs: In New York City, for example, a citizens' patrol called Thirteen Resolved to Evict All Dealers—Thread—was created in mid-1987 solely to rid a small area of Manhattan near the East River of crack dealers.

But some troubled neighborhoods across the country have invited larger groups to come in and push out drug dealers from the community. The best known are the Guardian Angels, a ten-year-old New York-based group whose membership has grown to several thousand as distant communities have enlisted their help. Welcomed by residents as saviors but condemned by many police officers as vigilantes operating on the edge of lawlessness, the Angels' job is to chase dealers from the area they are assigned to patrol. Easily identified by their red berets and white T-shirts, the Guardian Angels enter a community upon invitation of the residents and accept no money for their services. Angels patrol the streets unarmed, but they have been highly successful in disrupting the drug business in communities as diverse as New York City's Restaurant Row and Houston. Unhindered by rules of conduct required of police officers, who cannot apprehend suspects without probable cause, the Guardian Angels verbally harass and often physically oust drug dealers. They also make citizens' arrests of suspects, apprehending and holding them until police arrive.

Nation of Islam plays a similar role. Impeccably dressed in suits and bow ties and rigorously disciplined, the Muslims have been welcomed as positive role models for urban youth in neighborhoods of Brooklyn, New

York, and Washington, D.C., where they have successfully driven away drug dealers. But neither are the Muslims universally accepted. Their arrival in April 1988 at Mayfair Mansions, a low-income apartment complex in Washington that had served as a major crack market, met with controversy after they roughed up a television cameraman who was filming their patrol. Then-police chief Turner criticized the group as vigilantes.

Although the bad feelings between the police and the Muslim patrols later ebbed as the patrols uprooted the retail drug outlets from Mayfair Mansions, the controversy did not. Because neighborhood patrols cover a limited and usually well-defined area and have no power to bring dealers to justice, critics say, they merely drive the drug business to other, less protected neighborhoods. While Nation of Islam patrols were cleaning out Mayfair Mansions, residents of equally defenseless communities a few blocks away began to complain that drug dealers were taking over their streets.

Notes

1. General Accounting Office, *Controlling Drug Abuse: A Status Report* (Washington, D.C.: U.S. Government Printing Office, 1988).
2. Ann B. Wrobleski, letter to the editor, *Washington Post*, February 6, 1989, A10.
3. Alan Riding, "Rebels Disrupting the Eradication of Coca in Peru," *New York Times*, January 26, 1989, A10.
4. Rensselaer W. Lee III, "Dimensions of the South American Cocaine Industry" (Paper delivered at the Latin American Narcotics Trade and United States National Security conference, Mississippi State University, June 16-17, 1988), 31.
5. Thornburgh announced the results of the International Drug Enforcement Conference's activities August 30, 1988. The coalition includes the United States, Argentina, Belize, Bolivia, Brazil, Canada, Chile, Colombia, Costa Rica, the Dominican Republic, Ecuador, El Salvador, Guatemala, Honduras, Mexico, Panama, Paraguay, Peru, Uruguay, and Venezuela. Spain, Portugal, France, Belgium, the Netherlands, Britain, West Germany, Switzerland, and Italy also participated in the coalition's crackdown.
6. Major drug producing or drug transit countries are defined by the Foreign Assistance Act of 1961 as those that produce more than five metric tons of opium or opium derivatives, or more than 500 metric tons of marijuana, a year; those that are important sources of illicit or psychotropic drugs; those through which such drugs are transported; or those in which large amounts of drug money are laundered with the knowledge or complicity of the government. The twenty-four nations so identified in February 1987 were Afghanistan, the Bahamas, Belize, Bolivia, Brazil, Burma, Colombia, Ecuador, Hong Kong, India, Iran, Jamaica, Laos, Lebanon, Malaysia, Mexico, Morocco, Nigeria, Pakistan, Panama, Paraguay, Peru, Syria, and Thailand.
7. Ann B. Wrobleski testified June 1, 1988, before the House Government Operations Subcommittee on Government Information, Justice, and Agriculture.

8. Lee, "Dimensions of the South American Cocaine Industry," 27.
9. Title 10 of the U.S. Code, sections 371-379: "Military Cooperation with Civilian Law Enforcement Officials."
10. National Drug Enforcement Policy Board, *National and International Drug Law Enforcement Strategy—Report to Congress,* January 20, 1987.
11. U.S. General Accounting Office, *Drug Interdiction: Operation Autumn Harvest: A National Guard-Customs Anti-Smuggling Effort,* GAO/GGD-88-86, June 1988, 5.
12. Michael Isikoff, "Drug Fighters Resist Unifying, Senators Say," *Washington Post,* September 16, 1988, A25.
13. Peter Reuter, "Can the Borders Be Sealed?" *Public Interest* (Summer 1988): 53.
14. William M. Carley, "Losing Battle: U.S. Air War on Drugs So Far Fails to Stem Caribbean Smuggling," *Wall Street Journal,* October 20, 1988, 1.
15. National Drug Enforcement Policy Board, *The Cannabis Problem—Historical Overview: An Analysis of the Domestic Cannabis Problem and the Federal Response,* August 1986.
16. Ibid., 41.
17. U.S. Congress, House, Committee on Government Operations, H.R. 100-454, *Going to Pot: Marijuana Cultivation on Public Lands and the Federal Response,* 100th Cong., 1st sess., November 20, 1987, 13.
18. Charles P. Smith testified June 1, 1988, before the House Government Operations Subcommittee on Government Information, Justice, and Agriculture.
19. Marshall Ingwerson, "Rise in Drug Offenses Crams Prisons," *Christian Science Monitor,* December 13, 1988, 3.
20. Mary Jordan, "Most Tough Va. Drug Bills Killed," *Washington Post,* February 23, 1989, D5.
21. Gordon Witkin, "Hitting Kingpins in Their Assets," *U.S. News and World Report,* December 5, 1988, 20-22.
22. William Overend, "Expensive Residues of Crumbled Cocaine Empire Seized by U.S.," *Los Angeles Times,* August 22, 1988, 3.
23. Todd S. Purdum, "Koch Assails Program That Evicts Innocent Occupants in Drug Raids," *New York Times,* January 8, 1989, 25.
24. Timothy Egan, "U.S. Agents Aid Drug Fight in Seattle," *New York Times,* July 15, 1988, 6.

8 Policy Options for Dealing with Demand

As we have seen, even the most drastic supply-side policy measures have failed to pose an appreciable obstacle to the drug trade. From eradication at the source, to intercepting traffic outside the United States, to interdiction at the border, to law enforcement at home and even last-ditch vigilantism in the streets, nothing has worked. Indeed, the availability of the most popular harmful drug—crack cocaine—has become even more widespread. Even as the war on drugs reached its most fevered pitch to date, supply has increased and prices have gone down.

But what about the other side of the economic equation, consumer demand for the products of the drug business? Producer-nation governments, which have come under fire from Congress for their role in America's drug problem, have been especially vocal in pointing out the need to reduce demand. The government of Colombia has taken out full-page advertisements in U.S. newspapers to present its case: "Without demand there is no supply. That is a simple law of economics. And more than 50% of the world's illegal cocaine is consumed in the U.S. The plain truth is we will never win this war without the support of every American. The menace will not go away until demand goes away." [1]

Producer nations are not alone in their plea. In a recent report on several problems that are undermining U.S.-Latin America relations, the Inter-American Dialogue, an independent organization of prominent citizens of North, Central, and South America, concludes, "Until the United States curbs its demand for narcotics, traffickers will always be one step ahead of supply-side policies, leaving governments of the Hemisphere pursuing a will-of-the-wisp." [2]

Policy makers can use several approaches to dampen demand for illegal drugs. Seen as "carrot and stick" elements to policy, carrots include education, aimed at preventing potential consumers from taking up drugs in the first place, and, for consumers who already abuse or are addicted to drugs, treatment and rehabilitation. Sticks include harsh laws aimed at drug users.

To the extent that it has focused on the demand side at all, the U.S. government has placed the greatest emphasis on law enforcement. The Reagan administration heeded the advice of some critics of the supply-side bias evident in previous drug-enforcement policy. Frustrated by the relentless spread of the drug business in the 1980s, some began calling for stricter measures, even mandatory jail sentences for casual drug users, to raise the risks of buying banned substances. Only by adopting such a "user prosecution" strategy, it was said, would demand fall and thus also the profit margins of drug dealers. "By raising the risk of incarceration for both casual and hard-core users of drugs, we would greatly damp the demand for the illegal substances," wrote Joseph Perkins, an editorial writer for the *Wall Street Journal*. "By reducing demand, we would lower the profit margin for sellers, who would also face a 'higher cost of doing business' in the form of prison time themselves. With lower profit margins in drugs, sellers may actually find legal commerce more lucrative."[3]

Some local enforcement agencies had already adopted the user-prosecution strategy. Peter Nunez, U.S. attorney for the Southern District of California, began a program in 1987 under which anyone found to possess any amount of drugs is subject to arrest. While few users have actually spent time in jail under the program, drug possession results in probation or deferred prosecution, depending on the suspect's subsequent record. Other states and localities have adopted their own versions of user-prosecution laws. In New Jersey, for example, anyone possessing drugs loses his driver's license for at least six months and faces a fine and mandatory community service. In an effort to deter youths under sixteen from using drugs, the state can delay issuing a driver's license for as long as a year. Since 1986 the Miami Task Force Street Narcotics Detail has practiced a form of user prosecution that has since been emulated in many other cities. In an operation called the "reverse sting," undercover agents first arrest a street-level dealer, then pose as his substitute and arrest anyone who tries to buy drugs from him.

On March 21, 1988 the Reagan administration took the biggest step to date in the direction of user accountability when it introduced its so-called zero-tolerance program. Edwin Meese, then chairman of the administration's National Drug Policy Board, proclaimed there was "no such thing as recreational drug use" and urged state and local prosecutors to crack down on the users as well as the sellers of illegal drugs, treating the possession of even minute quantities as a major offense. Federal agents were instructed to seize vessels within twelve miles of the coastline if they found any banned substances on board. Ostensibly aimed at reducing the supply of imported drugs, zero-tolerance also targeted casual users of small amounts of banned substances, including marijuana.

Several well-publicized confiscations prompted an uproar over zero-tolerance. In May the coast guard seized the *Ark Royal*, a $2.5 million yacht, in international waters off the coast of Mexico after agents discovered a tenth of an ounce of marijuana on board. Customs service agents also seized the *Atlantis II*, the country's most sophisticated research ship, owned by the Woods Hole Oceanographic Institution in Massachusetts, after they found a trace of marijuana on board. Owners of commercial fishing vessels complained that the seizure policy was unfair because it made them pay for the behavior of employees they could not control. Critics called the new policy simple harassment whose victims often were innocent of any wrongdoing.

Bowing to public pressure, the administration relaxed zero-tolerance barely two months after it was introduced, barring the coast guard from seizing vessels in international waters unless there is evidence of smuggling activity. But inside U.S. territorial waters, within twelve miles of the coastline, the policy of confiscating vessels with even minimal traces of banned substances remains in effect. Congress further relaxed the seizure provisions of zero-tolerance with a law requiring the government to return seized vehicles and boats to owners who can prove they were unaware that drugs were present at the time of the search. Further, in early 1989 the customs service and the coast guard issued modified guidelines instructing their agents not to seize commercial fishing vessels found to carry as little as an ounce of marijuana or a gram of cocaine or heroin, amounts considered suitable only for personal use. Zero-tolerance policy was also expected to be relaxed for private craft.

Drug Testing Sparks Controversy

No aspect of government demand-side enforcement policy has sparked as much controversy in the late 1980s as drug testing. Certain government agencies that handle sensitive information, such as the CIA and the military, for years have been quietly testing employees and job applicants for drug use. The Transportation Department began testing civilian workers in 1986, while the Defense Department began screening new recruits in June 1988.

But it was the Reagan administration's crusade to attain a "drug-free workplace" that set off the most vocal protests. In September 1986 President Ronald Reagan issued an executive order requiring that federal workers be tested for use of illegal drugs. The army and the Transportation Department were allowed to institute testing programs immediately, while other agencies were required to devise appropriate policies to identify jobs that were sufficiently sensitive, for reasons of public safety or national security, to warrant screening. The federal guidelines issued in 1988 by the Department of Health and Human Services also require the tests to be conducted in a random fashion except in specific cases of suspected drug use.

Apart from the issue of constitutionality, critics of generalized drug testing question the program's cost-effectiveness. The federal government disbursed at least $15 million in initial expenses, while the army and the Transportation Department spent another $14 million to conduct their initial, two-year testing program. That program of random testing of current employees uncovered drug use among 203 federal workers, including sixty air traffic controllers and forty-two workers in nuclear and chemical weapons facilities. That amounts to drug use of 0.7 percent of the tested workers, a rate critics say is insignificant. They also point out that the vast majority of workers who tested positive did so for marijuana, and not the more debilitating drugs such as cocaine, heroin, or PCP. And, because marijuana can be traced in the urine for up to two months after its use, critics say the tests cannot uncover the use of illegal substances at the workplace.[4]

Federal workers, led by unions and the American Civil Liberties Union (ACLU), have challenged drug testing in at least fourteen lawsuits, but the courts remain divided on the issue. The principle yet to be decided is whether testing violates the Fourth Amendment to the Constitution, which prohibits unreasonable search and seizure. Critics contend that urine testing amounts to a bodily search. According to Ira Glasser, executive director of the ACLU,

> The constitutional amendment struck a reasonable balance between privacy and law enforcement. The police would be able to search people, but only if there was good reason to believe that a particular individual was involved in a crime or possessed evidence of a crime. . . . You can't search everyone, innocent and guilty alike, to find a few who are guilty. This basic American principle has been abandoned by those who advocate urine tests for everyone.[5]

The least controversial drug-testing programs are those that restrict testing to employees suspected of illegal drug use. Other programs screen all workers periodically or only prospective employees. Post-accident testing is restricted to workers involved in the accident, such as the 1987 Conrail train wreck outside Baltimore, Maryland. The engineer of the train in that accident, in which sixteen people died, later admitted to having smoked marijuana on the job. Proponents of drug testing, especially random testing, say such incidents justify the programs. "First and foremost, testing identifies drug users so they can be removed from jobs where they pose an immediate threat to others," writes former transportation secretary Jim Burnley. "Second, the war on drugs cannot be won by simply throwing drug dealers in jail; it must be made clear that illegal drug use is unacceptable, and there will be immediate consequences for those who choose this reckless form of so-called recreation."[6]

Most controversial are the programs that conduct random testing. Recently, U.S. District Court Judge Harold H. Greene decided in favor of the National Federation of Federal Employees and the American Civil

Liberties Union who filed suit on behalf of 17,000 employees of the Interior Department and stopped the department's planned program to introduce random drug testing in January 1989. The Ninth U.S. Circuit Court of Appeals in San Francisco has also ruled in favor of the opponents of drug testing in several cases, including a Bureau of Prisons plan covering 13,000 federal prison employees. In December 1988, U.S. District Court Judge Marilyn Hall Patel stopped the Transportation Department from conducting random drug tests among four million transportation workers in the private sector, including bus and truck drivers, on the grounds that the tests would violate the workers' right to privacy. While the constitutional questions involved in random drug testing remain unresolved, the Supreme Court ruled in July 1989 that Transportation Department regulations requiring drug testing of railway workers are justified by the government's role in protecting public safety. It also upheld the customs service's drug-testing requirement for certain job categories in a case brought by the National Treasury Employees Union. Finally, the Court ruled that private railroads and airlines are not required to negotiate with unions before imposing mandatory drug testing as a part of employees' periodic physicals.

Insofar as they concern the constitutional principle of unreasonable search and seizure of federal employees alone, the Supreme Court decisions will not directly affect the workplace outside government. But they undoubtedly will have an impact on the private sector as well. Already, under a provision of a 1988 law, all federal agencies have issued regulations requiring private government contractors to maintain a drug-free workplace. Those that do not adhere to the regulations face losing their government contracts for as long as five years. In order to comply, contractors must adopt some type of employee drug awareness program.

By the time the regulations covering government contractors went into effect on March 18, 1989, however, most private employers had already introduced programs aimed at preventing or stopping drug use among employees. Nearly half had introduced employee drug-testing programs, while a third screened new workers, according to the American Management Association. But a Labor Department study issued January 11, 1989, reported that less than 1 percent of American workers were actually tested for drug use during the twelve-month period beginning in the summer of 1987. The report, the first nationwide survey of private sector drug testing programs, also found that the majority of testing programs had been adopted by large companies, such as General Motors and American Telephone & Telegraph, which employ about a fifth of the nation's work force. According to those findings, 9 percent of the workers tested for drug use tested positive.[7]

Treatment of Drug Abusers and Addicts

For all the controversy surrounding drug testing, programs put in place so far have uncovered only a very small part of the drug abuse problem. The National Institute on Drug Abuse (NIDA) estimates that about 23 million Americans used illicit drugs in 1985. Of these, more than 6.5 million were "severely dependent" on cocaine, amphetamines, heroin, and other opiates. By severely dependent, the agency means those who require special treatment to break their habit.[8]

Responding to the expanding drug epidemic, the federal government has nearly doubled spending on treatment programs, from $205 million in 1981 to $370 million in 1988. But this is only a small part of the funding requirement. Drug treatment and rehabilitation have been left largely to the states and local governments to set up, fund, and administer. As a consequence of the Reagan administration's "new federalism" campaign to shift the burden of many social programs from Washington to the states, the federal government picks up only a fifth of the cost of the nation's more than 3,000 drug treatment and rehabilitation facilities through federal "alcohol and drug treatment rehabilitation" block grants. Treatment programs absorb almost 80 percent of the funds spent by state-supported alcohol and drug abuse services, according to the State Alcohol and Drug Agency.

While the source of funds for drug treatment has shifted to state and local levels, the methods used to help addicts break their dependency have remained virtually unchanged. Since the 1960s, NIDA reports, four basic types of treatment have been used to help drug abusers break their habit. The first is methadone maintenance treatment, first introduced in the early 1960s in New York City by Drs. Vincent P. Dole and Marie Nyswander. Methadone is a synthetic opiate that, taken orally, can block an addict's urge for heroin. It is usually dispensed to addicts on an outpatient basis and is intended to reduce the high risks inherent in heroin use—criminal activity to fund the habit, exposure to street violence, risk of overdose, and contraction of AIDS through needle sharing. Another advantage of methadone maintenance is the drug's long-lasting effect. Addicts used to injecting heroin every few hours need take methadone only once a day or even less frequently.

Methadone maintenance for heroin addicts became more widely used when the Nixon administration expanded federal funding for methadone treatment programs. But this approach to drug addictions has been controversial from the start. Because some patients never shake their dependence on methadone, the treatment may merely replace one addiction with another. But supporters of methadone treatment say it stabilizes the addict's condition, relieving his craving in a legal and safe atmosphere and allowing him to benefit from other rehabilitation services and, occasionally, to overcome the dependency. NIDA estimates that three-quarters of patients on methadone maintenance do not use heroin while they undergo treatment.

Another treatment is detoxification. It differs from classic methadone treatment by gradually decreasing the dosage of methadone or other drug substitute with the aim of weaning the addict from his dependency. Under the Narcotics and Addicts Treatment Act of 1974, detoxification programs using methadone were limited to twenty-one days. The maximum duration has since been extended to 180 days. But some experts say the regulations governing treatment with methadone should be further relaxed. In June 1988 the American Medical Association called for the federal government to expand treatment facilities and to allow private physicians to dispense methadone to narcotics addicts.[9] Current law treats such practice as a crime and allows only specially licensed clinics to offer methadone maintenance treatment. Further, methadone treatment is offered only to people who have been addicted to heroin for at least a year.

A third treatment involves long-term abstinence from drugs in the controlled environment of residential treatment centers. Often lasting more than a year, these therapeutic programs combine counseling and support group activities designed to help addicts change the antisocial and unproductive behavior that led to drug abuse in the first place. One of the best-known residential programs is an eighteen-month treatment offered by Phoenix House in New York City. Another is Karrick Hall, a residential treatment center run by the Bureau of Alcoholism Treatment Service in Washington, D.C. The center treats drug addicts using the same techniques it uses for alcoholics, by insisting on abstinence while educating patients to assume responsibility for their behavior.

Finally, there are drug-free outpatient programs designed to help people who are dependent on different types of substances. These include daytime therapeutic activities, group therapy, and recreational activities. Some of the fastest-growing outpatient programs are Narcotics Anonymous and Cocaine Anonymous, volunteer self-help groups patterned after Alcoholics Anonymous that provide support for recovering drug addicts. Similarly, Co-Anon was founded in the mid-1980s to help families of cocaine addicts in much the same way Al-Anon helps families of alcoholics change the behavior patterns that have contributed to their family member's addiction, a phenomenon known as co-dependency. All these groups share the goal of helping addicts stay off drugs after their initial treatment. Not substitutes for more intensive treatment, they are generally helpful only to drug users who are to some extent functioning again in society, such as those who have completed long-term residential programs.

The widespread availability of cheap and highly addictive crack poses a daunting challenge to these traditional approaches to drug treatment. Many heroin users, for example, also use crack and other drugs. Such "polyaddicts" respond poorly to methadone treatment because the synthetic narcotic does nothing to reduce the craving for the other substances. Further, while crack may be more addictive than heroin, there is no known chemical substitute that can reproduce crack's euphoric effect as methadone does for heroin addicts. For this reason, most crack users who submit to traditional drug treatment, including psychotherapy and residential treatment, suffer relapses within weeks or months. From the cocaine addict's point of view, a fundamental flaw in existing treatment programs is the lack of adequate space to obtain treatment on demand. Because crack addicts require instant gratification, only immediate access to treatment is a realistic alternative to a "fix." But waiting lists at public drug-treatment facilities in most cities are long, some as long as two years. While private residential treatment centers may have room, few crack addicts—typically young, poor, and unemployed—can afford the price of treatment, which can exceed $10,000 a month.

Because crack addiction does not lend itself to traditional drug treatment methods, some drug abuse experts have called for a major nationwide research effort to find a pharmacological answer to the problem. "Without such a commitment to cocaine treatment research, any hope we have of stemming the national epidemic of substance abuse and its concomitant medical and social problems will be as insubstantial as the smoke from a crack pipe," writes Stephen C. Joseph, New York City's commissioner of health.[10]

In 1988 research on a "methadone clone" to treat cocaine addiction yielded some promising results. Dr. Frank H. Gawin of Yale University's School of Medicine found that desipramine, an antidepressant, reduces the craving for cocaine and could help crack addicts abstain from the drug for three to four weeks. Researchers at the University of Minnesota School of Medicine obtained similar results using another antidepressant, carbamazepine, which has also been used to prevent convulsive seizures. While these drugs helped reduce the intense craving for cocaine, federal government researchers working at the Addiction Research Center in Baltimore found they could reduce crack-induced euphoria by administering calcium channel blockers, which prevent the passage of calcium into and out of cells.[11] None of these "methadone clones" is expected to relieve cocaine addicts of their dependency, but it is hoped that, like methadone for the heroin addict, they might relieve the intense craving long enough for addicts to seek rehabilitation treatment.

The shortage of drug treatment centers is especially severe for intravenous drug users, who are mostly heroin addicts but also cocaine users. The

National Association of State Alcohol and Drug Abuse Directors estimates there are 1.2 million IV drug abusers, but only 150,000 persons currently in drug treatment programs. More than a million other IV users should receive treatment, about a third of whom the association estimates would be willing to do so if it were available. Assuming a $5,000 annual drug treatment cost per person, the association calculates that it would cost an additional $1.8 billion a year to meet the demand for treatment by America's IV drug users.

City governments, especially in Washington and New York, have come under fire for failing to open more drug treatment and rehabilitation clinics. Beset with financial strains caused in large part by the drug epidemic, cities have tended to emphasize law enforcement, hiring more police officers to try to stem the violence that accompanies drug sales. Thus, although New York governor Mario Cuomo promised to provide drug treatment programs for 5,500 more people by March 1990, critics doubted that the state would find the necessary funds to expand its program, which currently treats more than 47,000 people. While Washington mayor Marion Barry promised to open more drug treatment centers as part of his citywide antidrug campaign, Operation Fight Back, the city's Alcohol and Drug Abuse Services Administration saw its budget cut by $2 million in 1989. Washington and other cities are also stymied by citizen resistance to opening more methadone and other treatment facilities; local residents fear they will merely bring the drug trade to their neighborhoods.

The need for expanded drug treatment and rehabilitation facilities has been more widely recognized with the spread of AIDS. Among its recommendations for policy changes needed to confront the AIDS epidemic, the Presidential Commission on the Human Immunodeficiency Virus Epidemic called for "a national policy of providing 'treatment on demand' for intravenous drug users." The commission predicted that such a program would cost $1.5 billion a year above current levels and recommended the spending be split evenly between the federal government and state and local governments. The commission strongly supported the various approaches that have been used to treat drug addiction and called for their expansion: "Current treatment modalities for intravenous drug abusers, including methadone maintenance and drug-free residential communities reduce illicit drug use, improve employment among addicts, reduce crime rates, and improve social functioning." [12]

Likewise, the Institute of Medicine of the National Academy of Sciences said "the most serious deficiency in current efforts to control HIV infection in the United States" was the "gross inadequacy of federal efforts to reduce HIV transmission among IV drug abusers." The organization's AIDS Activities Oversight Committee, in its 1988 update on efforts to combat AIDS, called for the "rapid, large-scale expansion of drug abuse treatment slots, both in residential drug-free treatment centers and in methadone maintenance facilities, to offer immediate access to all addicts who request treatment." [13]

Needle-Exchange Programs

The relationship between IV drug abuse and the spread of AIDS has prompted a search for nontraditional ways to treat drug addicts. In November 1988 New York City, where an estimated 60 percent of some 200,000 IV drug users are infected with AIDS, became the first U.S. city to use public money to fund a highly controversial needle-exchange program. Modeled after similar programs in Western Europe and Australia, New York's program—limited to 200 subjects—was introduced as an experimental study to determine whether the spread of AIDS among IV drug users can be slowed. Some of the European programs, notably a four-year-old needle exchange in Amsterdam, appear to have slowed the spread of AIDS, and none appear to have resulted in increased drug use.

The New York City health commissioner and other proponents of the program say it may not only slow the spread of AIDS but also help addicts break their habit. In recognition of concern that the program might seem to support drug abuse, there are several strict requirements for participation. Only addicts who are on waiting lists at drug-treatment centers are accepted into the program. To obtain clean needles, they must first turn in their used needles to the Health Department. As an incentive to join the program, participating addicts are given priority placement in drug-treatment programs. The program has the support of both former surgeon general C. Everett Koop and the National Academy of Sciences, which conducts periodic AIDS surveys.

The needle exchange has also sparked debate over New York's ban on over-the-counter sales of hypodermic needles and syringes. Where they are legally sold, hypodermic needles cost as little as 20 cents apiece. But because it is illegal to possess needles without a prescription in New York, their street price is about $5, too expensive for addicts whose first priority is to buy drugs. They tend to share or rent the needles, or "works," in the shooting galleries where they buy drugs. Critics of the needle ban in New York and eleven other states as well as the District of Columbia say it does nothing to deter drug use while making it harder to stop the spread of AIDS. The New York County Lawyers Association has estimated that the rate of HIV infection among IV drug users is 31 percent in states that prohibit the sale of needles but only 5 percent in states where their sale is legal.[14]

But New York City's needle-sharing program is strongly opposed by prosecutors, some operators of drug treatment programs, school officials, and especially representatives of the black and Hispanic communities where IV drug use is prevalent. They say the needle exchange amounts to tacit acceptance of drug abuse among the minority population and may actually encourage people to take up the habit by making the paraphernalia more readily available. Critics point out that heroin, the drug of choice among IV drug users, causes painful withdrawal symptoms, and that addicts are unlikely to discriminate between used and clean needles in their urgency to obtain a fix. They also say the program diverts public attention and funds from the city's woefully inadequate drug-treatment facilities.

Many big U.S. cities are awaiting the preliminary results of New York City's needle exchange to determine whether to institute similar government-sponsored programs. Meanwhile, privately supported needle exchanges are already operating in several smaller cities. A private clinic in Portland, Oregon, called OutsideIn, was set to start up a long-planned needle exchange program after it obtained liability insurance in early 1989. Although only 5 percent of the local IV drug users are thought to be infected with the AIDS virus, the city is an important point of entry for Mexican black tar heroin, and the program's supporters hoped to prevent a major outbreak by providing clean needles. In Tacoma, Washington, a drug counselor, with assistance from the local health department, has been giving out clean needles on demand since September 1988.

The Role of Education in Prevention

Whether or not needle exchanges succeed in slowing the spread of AIDS, critics remain adamant that any facilitation of drug use flies in the face of the fundamental goal of the war on drugs, to eliminate the use of illegal substances entirely. The best way to do that, most agree, is to prevent people, especially teenagers and children, from taking drugs in the first place (Table 8-1). The federal government increased its support for drug education and prevention programs from $117 million in 1981 to $454 million in 1988. Of that amount, $131 million went to programs offered in schools.

The most visible advocate of education to prevent drug use has been Nancy Reagan. Even while her husband's drug policy emphasized the supply side, the former first lady insisted on the primary importance of curtailing consumer demand for illegal substances. "Frankly, it is far easier for the United States to focus on coca fields grown by 300,000 *campesinos* in Peru than to shut down the dealer who can be found on the street corners of our cities," Mrs. Reagan told a committee of the United Nations General Assembly. "We need to educate a generation to 'just say no' to drugs."[15]

Table 8-1 Trends in Perceived Availability of Drugs, High School Seniors, 1975-1988

Question: "How difficult do you think it would be for you to get each of the following types of drugs, if you wanted some?"

Drug	1975	1976	1977	1978	1979	1980	1981	1982	1983	1984	1985	1986	1987	1988
Marijuana	87.8	87.4	87.9	87.8	90.1	89.0	89.2	88.5	86.2	84.6	85.5	85.2	84.8	85.0
Amyl & butyl nitrites	N/A	N/A	N/A	N/A	N/A	N/A	N/A	N/A	N/A	N/A	N/A	N/A	23.9	25.9
LSD	46.2	37.4	34.5	32.2	34.2	35.3	35.0	34.2	30.9	30.6	30.5	28.5	31.4	33.3
PCP	N/A	N/A	N/A	N/A	N/A	N/A	N/A	N/A	N/A	N/A	N/A	N/A	22.8	24.9
Other psychedelics	47.8	35.7	33.8	33.8	34.6	35.0	32.7	30.6	26.6	26.6	26.1	24.9	25.0	26.2
Cocaine	37.0	34.0	33.0	37.8	45.5	47.9	47.5	47.4	43.1	45.0	48.9	51.5	54.2	55.0
Crack	N/A	N/A	N/A	N/A	N/A	N/A	N/A	N/A	N/A	N/A	N/A	N/A	41.1	42.1
Cocaine powder	N/A	N/A	N/A	N/A	N/A	N/A	N/A	N/A	N/A	N/A	N/A	N/A	52.9	50.3
Heroin	24.2	18.4	17.9	16.4	18.9	21.2	19.2	20.8	19.3	19.9	21.0	22.0	23.7	28.0
Other narcotics (including methadone)	34.5	26.9	27.8	26.1	28.7	29.4	29.6	30.4	30.0	32.1	33.1	32.2	33.0	35.8
Amphetamines	67.8	61.8	58.1	58.5	59.9	61.3	69.5	70.8	68.5	68.2	66.4	64.3	64.5	63.9
Barbiturates	60.0	54.4	52.4	50.6	49.8	49.1	54.9	55.2	52.5	51.9	51.3	48.3	48.2	47.8
Tranquilizers	71.8	65.5	64.9	64.3	61.4	59.1	60.8	58.9	55.3	54.5	54.7	51.2	48.6	49.1

Note: Percentage saying drug would be "fairly easy" or "very easy" for them to get. Answer alternatives were (1) probably impossible, (2) very difficult, (3) fairly difficult, (4) fairly easy, and (5) very easy.

Source: L. D. Johnston, P. M. O'Malley, and J. G. Bachman, *Drug Use, Drinking, and Smoking: National Survey Results from High School, College, and Young Adult Populations*, U.S. Department of Health and Human Services, National Institute on Drug Abuse, 1989.

After launching her "Just Say No" campaign at a school in Oakland, California, in July 1984, Mrs. Reagan appeared across the country with her message that even casual experimentation with banned substances carries a heavy risk of addiction. Thousands of "Just Say No" clubs have been set up in schools to help children resist the temptation to try drugs. On the same model, private groups have set up education campaigns aimed at different groups. The Partnership for a Drug-Free America, for example, takes out full-page newspaper advertisements to inform adults of the risks involved in taking drugs and urges employers to force drug users among their work force to seek treatment.

Unfortunately, educational programs aimed at preventing adolescents from experimenting with drugs appear to have had little impact. Some appear even to have had the perverse effect of encouraging youths to try drugs out of curiosity or as a way to challenge authority. Other types of educational programs seek instead to help young people overcome personal problems, such as low self-esteem and difficulty resisting peer pressure, which make some more vulnerable than others to the lure of drugs. One such program, Drug Abuse Resistance Education, or DARE, founded in Los Angeles in 1983, has been introduced to an estimated 1.5 million children in elementary and intermediate schools across the country. Former education secretary William Bennett, later appointed the nation's first "drug czar," was outspoken in his support for DARE and similar programs, in which local police departments participate by sending officers to teach classes in the schools.[16]

A further blow to educational drug-prevention schemes has been dealt by recent studies indicating that occasional drug use among teenagers may cause no long-term effects, and certainly not the debilitating damage suffered by chronic drug users. A study released by the University of California at Los Angeles in July 1988 questioned the usefulness of educational programs such as Mrs. Reagan's "Just Say No" campaign that aim to prevent first-time use. The massive study of adolescent drug patterns, supported by the National Institute on Drug Abuse, concluded that programs should instead inform youth of the dangers of the "abuse, regular use, and misuse" of drugs.[17]

Notes

1. Advertisement in *Washington Post*, October 14, 1988.
2. Aspen Institute for Humanistic Studies, *The Americas in 1988: A Time for Choices: A Report of the Inter-American Dialogue*, May 1988, 42.
3. Joseph Perkins, "How to Put Drug Dealers out of Business," *Wall Street Journal*, May 26, 1988, 26.
4. Judith Havemann, "Drug Tests Catch 203 in Sensitive Jobs," *Washington Post*, March 8, 1989, A1.

5. Ira Glasser, "A Question of Privacy," in *The Drug Testing Debate: Remedy or Reaction* (Washington, D.C.: American Federation of State, County, and Municipal Employees, 1987), 11-12.
6. Jim Burnley, "With So Many Crashes, Drug Tests Are Worth It," *Washington Post*, November 26, 1988, A21.
7. See Andrew Kupfer, "Is Drug Testing Good or Bad?" *Fortune*, December 19, 1988, 133-40.
8. National Institute on Drug Abuse, "Drug Abuse Treatment," *NIDA Capsules* (Rockville, Md.: U.S. Department of Health and Human Services, June 1988).
9. For a description of this view, see Donald R. Wesson, "Revival of Medical Maintenance in the Treatment of Heroin Dependence," *Journal of the American Medical Association* (June 10, 1988): 3314-15.
10. Stephen C. Joseph, "A Methadone Clone for Cocaine," *New York Times*, January 11, 1989, A23.
11. Larry Thompson, "Curbing the Craving for Cocaine," *Washington Post* (Health section), February 21, 1989, 9.
12. Presidential Commission on the Human Immunodeficiency Virus Epidemic, Chairman's Draft Recommendations for the Final Report, June 2, 1988, 146.
13. Institute of Medicine, National Academy of Sciences, *Confronting AIDS: Update 1988* (Washington, D.C.: National Academy of Sciences, 1988), 41.
14. Chris Anne Raymond, "U.S. Cities Struggle to Implement Needle Exchanges Despite Apparent Success in European Cities," *Journal of the American Medical Association* (November 11, 1988): 2620-21.
15. Cited by Paul Lewis, "Nancy Reagan, at U.N., Says U.S. Must Do More to Combat Drugs," *New York Times*, October 26, 1988, A1.
16. U.S. Department of Education, *What Works: Schools without Drugs* (Washington, D.C.: U.S. Government Printing Office, 1987).
17. Janny Scott, "UCLA Study on Drug Use Rekindles Debate on Risk," *Los Angeles Times*, August 10, 1988, 1.

9 The War on Drugs at the End of the 1980s

Pressed by their constituents' growing frustration with the government's apparent inability to curtail the drug trade, Congress followed up on the massive Anti-Drug Abuse Act of 1986 with an even more sweeping drug law in 1988. The measure, which dominated the legislative agenda in that election year, included many drastic law-enforcement provisions attached by members who were eager to appear tough on drugs to voters back home. By the time House and Senate conferees agreed on the final version of the law, the last piece of legislation the 100th Congress acted on, many of the more extreme provisions had been dropped.

Passed on October 22, the Anti-Drug Abuse Act of 1988 was signed into law by President Ronald Reagan on November 18. It authorized an unprecedented $2.8 billion over the $3.5 billion spent in 1988 to combat the war on drugs. It also created a new position for a "drug czar" to oversee and coordinate the actions of the thirty-three federal agencies involved in drug enforcement. The law's most evident bow to voter frustration over the expanding business of illegal drugs was a provision allowing, but not mandating, the death penalty in drug-related murders, as well as stiff penalties against recreational drug users, estimated at some twenty-three million Americans. The new law also calls for more spending on interdiction and other supply-side efforts aimed at keeping drugs from getting into the United States in the first place (Table 9-1). It increased law-enforcement aid to Latin American countries and mandated foreign-aid sanctions against governments that do not cooperate in antidrug programs. The law also increased penalties against dealers in the United States and permitted courts to suspend federal benefits, such as public housing and college loans, for people convicted of drug crimes. In an attempt to cut recreational drug consumption, it allows courts to impose civil fines and penalties, including the revocation of passports and drivers' licenses, against people caught with small amounts of banned substances.

Some critics of existing drug policy hailed the new law for its shift in emphasis from the supply side to the demand side of the market for illicit drugs. Unlike previous legislation, which poured about three-quarters of drug policy funds into interdiction and enforcement, the 1988 law earmarked about 60 percent of new funding for treatment and prevention,

Table 9-1 International Narcotics Control Program Fiscal Summary (in thousands of dollars)

Country/program	FY 1988 enacted	FY 1989 estimate	FY 1990 request
Latin America			
Bolivia	$15,000[a]	$ 10,000	$ 9,200
Brazil	2,340	200	1,900
Colombia	9,767	10,000	10,000
Ecuador	1,000	1,000	1,400
Jamaica	1,900	1,000	1,900
Mexico	14,500	15,000	15,000
Peru	7,500	10,000	10,000
Venezuela	—	700	1,000
Latin America regional	7,000	7,000[b]	7,000
Subtotal	59,007	54,900	57,400
East Asia			
Burma	5,000	3,000	7,500
Thailand	3,935	3,900	3,500
Subtotal	8,935	6,900	11,000
Southwest Asia			
Pakistan	5,075	5,300	5,700
Turkey	350	350	350
Asia/Africa regional	369	450	450
Subtotal	5,794	6,100	6,500
Interregional aviation support	13,414	22,700	28,000
Total country programs	87,150	90,600	102,900
International organizations	3,100	1,100	3,100
Interregional training and demand reduction	5,200	6,000	5,500
Program development and support	3,300	3,300	3,500
Total INM program	$98,750	$101,000	$115,000

[a] The $15 million program budget for Bolivia was earmarked by Congress in its FY 1988 Continuing Resolution.

[b] The FY 1989 Foreign Assistance Act earmarked a $7 million program budget for Latin America regional.

Source: U.S. Department of State, Bureau of International Narcotics Matters, *International Narcotics Control Strategy Report*, March 1989.

including education. Although experts continue to disagree over what kinds of educational programs actually work, many see education as the only effective way to cut consumer demand. The law also broke new ground by making treatment on demand an explicit goal of federal drug policy and by authorizing federal funds for treatment centers.

But, as critics were quick to point out, the 1988 drug law was more bluster than substance. Although it authorized an additional $2.8 billion for the drug effort over two years, the law actually appropriated only about $500 million in new spending during fiscal 1989. A larger appropriation would have pushed the federal budget deficit above the $146 billion ceiling imposed by the Gramm-Rudman-Hollings Act and triggered across-the-board spending cuts.

President George Bush, who in 1988 called for tougher sanctions against anyone involved in the business of drugs, continued his hard-line stance once in office. "Take my word for it," he declared in his inaugural address, "This scourge will stop." At the same time, Bush also supported the shift toward curtailing demand that is embodied in the new law. "The answer to the problem of drugs lies more on solving the demand side of the equation than it does on the supply side, than it does on interdiction or sealing the borders or something of that nature," Bush said a few days after his inauguration. "And so it is going to have to be a major educational effort, and the private sector and the schools are all going to have to be involved in this."[1]

Accordingly, Bush called for new spending of $947 million to fight drug abuse in his budget proposal for fiscal 1990. He specified that public treatment facilities and in-school educational programs would receive some of the new money. But he also proposed more spending for measures to slow the supply of drugs, including interdiction. Bush proposed an additional $318 million for Justice Department and prison programs aimed at toughening prosecution of dealers. "I also want to make sure that, when a drug dealer is convicted, there is a cell waiting for him. He should not go free because prisons are too full," Bush told a joint session of Congress.[2]

But Bush ran into trouble early in his stint as commander-in-chief of the war on drugs. His appointment of William Bennett as the first director of national drug control policy was opposed by some because of Bennett's lack of law-enforcement experience and his conservative political stance. Bennett, who actively campaigned for the appointment, was a highly controversial figure while serving as secretary of education during the last three and one-half years of the Reagan administration. His abrasive style, critics said, would hinder his ability to smooth relations among the thirty-three federal agencies involved in drug policy, one of the drug czar's main functions. In 1988, for example, Bennett called for the use of the military in controlling the supply of drugs, a position that was strongly opposed by the Defense Department, one of the agencies now within his domain.

Months after Bennett's appointment, it remained unclear just how much power the drug czar would be able to wield in his effort to coordinate drug policy. Bush further complicated the new director's job by declining to include Bennett among the members of his cabinet or his National Security Council (NSC), although the law that created the position stipulated that it would be "cabinet-level" and that the director should participate in NSC meetings. For his part, Bennett remained ambiguous on the direction his agency would take as he prepared the overall drug strategy the law required him to present to the president by September 1989.

Bennett did not wait six months, however, before taking action in certain aspects of the drug business. The day after he was confirmed by the Senate, Bennett singled out areas of the country in urgent need of special law-enforcement support as "high-intensity drug trafficking areas." With his declaration, Bennett made available federal grants to hire additional police officers, allowed for the federal appointment of additional prosecutors and judges to local courts, and ordered the transfer of prisoners from city jails to federal prisons to free up space for drug criminals. Also, on Bennett's recommendation, the Bush administration banned the importation of assault-type semiautomatic rifles, the weapons of choice among drug dealers.

Bennett's long-awaited drug strategy proved to be less dramatic than anticipated. Announced on September 5 by President Bush in his first nationally televised address as president, the plan kept in place the previous administration's focus on law enforcement in the government's war on drugs. True to his promise, Bush said the new policy would place less emphasis on the interdiction of drug imports at the nation's borders than before. But Bush's drug strategy does not reflect the kind of dramatic shift of resources from the supply side of the drug market to the demand side he had supported in earlier pronouncements. The new plan called for greater law enforcement efforts to arrest and punish both drug sellers and users. In this way, Bush appeared to have merely redrawn the main battle line of the war on drugs from the borders to the streets.

Critics of the new strategy also pointed to the lack of adequate funding to carry it out. While Bush said $7.9 billion would be needed to pay for his drug plan in 1990, he asked Congress for only $717 million in new funds. Congressional Democrats complained that the administration was trying to look like anti-drug warriors while at the same time refusing to pay the necessary price—by raising taxes if necessary—to achieve victory. "The president says he wants to wage a war on drugs, but if that's true, what we need is another D-Day, not another Vietnam, not a limited war, fought on the cheap, and destined for stalemate and human tragedy," said Sen. Joseph R. Biden, Jr., D-Del., in a televised response to the president's address.

Legalization: Surrender or Solution?

While the Bush administration calls for a continuing escalation of the war on drugs, few observers predict its policy will impede the flourishing drug trade. Such frustration with policy efforts to disrupt the supply of or the demand for banned substances is widespread and has led many experts and policy makers to question the wisdom of outlawing an industry whose products are so readily available and in such heavy demand.

Until recently, the suggestion that drugs be legalized was widely considered an extremist and immoral solution to the problem of illegal substances. This is still the official position enunciated by federal policy makers and law-enforcement agents. "It is time we as a nation quit talking about throwing in the towel—that's just not the American way," wrote William von Raab, former commissioner of the U.S. Customs Service. "What we must do is look for additional ways to punish drug traffickers and users alike, and take steps to put some meaning back into the lives of those who are so easily attracted to the death grip of drugs." [3]

The call for legalization, or decriminalization, of the drug trade is not new. But until recently, the legalization banner was carried by only a few disparate proponents, including libertarians, advocates of separate treatment of marijuana, and some conservative economists. Among the latter, Milton Friedman has called for an end to drug prohibition since 1972.[4] But in 1988, as frustration over the failure to curtail the drug boom mounted, more voices joined the call for legalization. These represented a wide range of political opinion, from *The Economist* magazine of London, an authoritative, mainstream conservative publication, to some liberal U.S. politicians, notably Baltimore mayor Kurt L. Schmoke, who came out in support of legalization and called for a nationwide debate on the issue.[5] For the first time ever, drug legalization was the subject of congressional hearings held in September 1988.[6]

Most proponents of drug legalization justify their position on the ample evidence that criminalization under the present system simply has not worked. They also point out the inconsistency of banning some mind-altering and potentially addictive substances while allowing others, chiefly tobacco and alcohol, to be produced, sold, and consumed freely. They cite the similarities between the war on drugs and Prohibition, the nation's other vast experiment with disrupting a thriving industry in mind-altering substances. They say that Prohibition, which lasted from 1919 to 1933, should have taught us that banning such goods merely pushes underground the industry that produces and sells them and promotes criminal behavior. The dealers running crack houses and the soaring sidewalk homicides of the 1980s, they say, are nothing more than modern versions of the bootleggers and gangland slayings of a half-century ago. Then, the criminal activities associated with the illegal alcohol industry ceased abruptly with the repeal of the Eighteenth Amendment.

Some critics of the war on drugs say the issue has been clouded by the failure to distinguish between the health problem of drug abuse and addiction and the broader effects of a legal ban on drugs. This is the challenge posed by some experts, including Ethan A. Nadelmann of Princeton University.[7] As evidence of drug prohibition's failure as public policy, he points out that the intended beneficiaries of the war on drugs—potential abusers—are actually its main victims, while the people drug prohibition is supposed to penalize—drug producers and traffickers—benefit from the high profits their goods command on the black market.

Not only does prohibition distort the intent of the law, critics say; it lacks the necessary moral support among the public at large. In the words of Stephen J. Morse, a professor at the University of Southern California Law Center, "We are fighting an enemy that large numbers of Americans do not consider their foe." [8] He goes on to cite drug user statistics to support his point, including eighteen million regular pot smokers, not to mention the uncounted numbers of people involved in the production of drugs outside the country who derive economic benefits from the drug trade.

Legalization of drugs, proponents emphasize, need not mean removing all barriers to free access to dangerous substances. Just as the individual states restrict the sale of alcohol by age and location, steps could be taken to keep dangerous drugs such as heroin and cocaine out of the hands of children. A regulatory framework might also be tailored to make it harder to obtain cocaine and heroin, for example, than it would be to buy marijuana. The Netherlands, for example, has allowed limited sales of marijuana in Amsterdam's coffee houses since 1976 while banning the sale of hard drugs. The country's heroin addicts are treated as patients rather than as criminals, and receive methadone maintenance treatment on demand.

The rationale for treating different segments of the drug industry in different ways is provided by a report on Dutch drug policy provided by the Netherlands embassy in Washington, D.C.

> If young people experimenting with cannabis products, which are relatively speaking less dangerous, have to rely on a black market which also deals in drugs with an unacceptable risk, there is a considerable danger of them changing over to the more dangerous drugs. Policy is therefore directed at separating the markets for the two kinds of drugs by adopting a lenient stance towards small-scale dealing in cannabis products (in 'coffee shops' for example) while at the same time taking every measure possible to restrict trafficking in drugs with an unacceptable risk. This approach largely keeps cannabis out of the serious crime sphere and is believed to help break down the mythology surrounding

> the use of drugs so that they become less attractive to young people. The situation in which users 'go underground' can then be avoided.[9]

Still, some respond that foreign experience does not provide a reliable guide to formulating U.S. policy. They point out that Dutch society is more homogeneous than American society and is confined to a smaller area that is more amenable to a flexible drug-enforcement policy. Moreover, not all experiments with legalization in other countries have succeeded in destroying the criminality associated with the drug trade. Britain's drug abuse policy, which has since the 1920s allowed physicians to dispense heroin to addicts, is commonly cited as an example of legalization's shortcomings. In the 1960s the policy came under attack as addiction sharply increased, partly because of corrupt physicians who sold heroin on the black market. The underground heroin trade eventually revived, and today Britain suffers from widespread heroin addiction and a thriving black market for the drug.

Supporters of decriminalization insist, though, that U.S. policy makers can learn from the experience of other countries to make some form of legalization work. Marijuana, they say, presents the most convincing case for repeal of existing drug laws because it is less dangerous than either tobacco or alcohol. Decriminalization of marijuana in about a dozen states during the late 1970s, Nadelmann writes, was not followed by increased use of the drug. Under Schmoke's proposal, marijuana use would be legalized, while heroin and cocaine would be distributed by physicians to addicts only. "If we're going to have a new war on drugs," he told the House Select Committee on Narcotics Abuse and Control, "let it be led by the surgeon general, not the attorney general." Interestingly, the group that has campaigned longer than any other for the legalization of a banned substance, the National Organization for the Reform of Marijuana Laws (NORML), opposes decriminalization of cocaine. Instead, NORML calls for the legalization of marijuana and taxation of the drug's sales (Figure 9-1). Those revenues could then be used to pay for better public education of the dangers posed by more dangerous drugs.

NORML's campaign received a boost from unexpected quarters in September 1988 when Francis L. Young, chief administrative law judge for the Drug Enforcement Agency, called for marijuana's legalization for medical purposes. The ruling culminated proceedings that had begun in 1972 when NORML first petitioned DEA to allow the use of marijuana as a prescription drug. Calling marijuana "one of the safest therapeutically active substances known to man," Young proposed that it be reclassified under the 1970 Controlled Substances Act so that physicians could prescribe it to treat certain conditions. If DEA redefined marijuana as a Schedule 2 substance (one approved for medical purposes), physicians would be allowed to prescribe the drug for specified medical uses.

Figure 9-1 Estimated Harvest Value of Marijuana by State (in millions of dollars)

Note: No figures were available for Delaware, Nevada, North Dakota, Rhode Island, and South Dakota.

Source: National Organization for the Reform of Marijuana Laws, 1987.

Ironically, cocaine and morphine are currently classified as Schedule 2 substances, while marijuana is included with PCP, LSD, and heroin in the most heavily restricted Schedule 1 category, for which all uses are banned. Marijuana has been found to counter the vomiting and weight loss that afflict cancer patients undergoing chemotherapy and to relieve symptoms of multiple sclerosis, spasticity, and glaucoma. Considering the prevailing militant view on all banned substances, however, DEA administrator John C. Lawn was not expected to act on Young's nonbinding recommendation. So supporters of the medical use of pot were expected to take their case back to the courts.

No matter how many currently banned substances were included, decriminalization would have several immediate effects. One of the main benefits would be to bring the industry into the legal economy, where profits could be taxed and access to dangerous substances could be more efficiently controlled. Decriminalization would also free up more than $100 billion now submerged in the underground economy. By removing the risks involved in the smuggling and sale of illegal drugs, legalization would deflate prices for these products, force many dealers to find legal employment, and eliminate the incentive for the deadly turf wars that accompany the current crack trade. "It is money that drives the drug trade, and the money was put there by the war on drugs," writes Pat M. Holt, a former chief of staff of the Senate Foreign Relations Committee. "So what needs to be done is to take the money out. . . . Paradoxically, drugs would be easier to control if they were cheap, safe, and easy to get—say at the corner drugstore." Holt went on to point out that the spread of AIDS by IV drug users would be easier to slow because addicts would have no reason to use dirty needles, the main vehicle of the disease's spread among that population.

Like their counterparts of the temperance movement, opponents of drug legalization say it would greatly increase drug abuse and addiction in the United States, creating "a nation of zombies," in the words of Sen. Alfonse M. D'Amato, R-N.Y. To justify their stance, they too point to Prohibition, citing the marked fall in alcoholism while the ban was in effect. No sooner was it repealed than the number of alcoholics increased again. Many advocates of drug decriminalization concede that drug abuse would probably spread during the initial period as drugs became more readily available, even if their sale were heavily regulated.

The legalization debate has divided the black community. On the one side are political leaders such as Schmoke and Washington mayor Marion Barry, who while not openly advocating legalization has called for discussions of alternatives to current policy. On the other side are those who say the war on drugs must be intensified to prevent the black community from being destroyed by the drug trade. Rep. Charles B.

Rangel, D-N.Y., chairman of the House narcotics panel, opened the legalization hearings declaring, "I am stringently opposed to anything approaching the legalization of illicit narcotics." He pointed to statistics indicating that while blacks make up only 11 percent of the population, one out of every three crack users in New York is black. "Under conditions that would make drugs cheaper and more readily available—as legalization would do—do we want to further these genocidal problems that we already have as a result of drug abuse?" Rangel queried.

But other experts, including Nadelmann, doubt this danger is as great as commonly thought. "There is good reason to assume that even if all the illegal drugs were made legally available, the same cultural restraints that now keep most Americans from becoming drug abusers would persist and perhaps even strengthen," Nadelmann writes.[10] Advocates of decriminalization also predict that as many drugs' harmful effects become more widely known, their use will eventually fall. Educational programs designed to inform the public of the risks of consuming dangerous substances would be a key ingredient of any legalization scheme. Modeled after Surgeon General C. Everett Koop's campaign to end cigarette smoking and alcohol abuse, such an effort would include heavy penalties imposed on anyone who caused injury or death while under the influence of any drug. Supporters of this alternative point to the success of education in dampening consumer demand for cigarettes, which are not only legally marketed but subsidized through federal funds paid to tobacco farmers. Although it took several decades for smokers to heed the evidence linking smoking to lung cancer and other diseases, the message has finally paid off, as fewer people are taking up the habit and smoking is less tolerated in public areas.[11]

Drugs Foster a Two-Tiered Society

It remains uncertain how the American public's frustration with the booming business of illegal drugs will affect public policy. The legalization debate has heated up, and new voices have been added to the roster of advocates of decriminalizing drugs. But the debate has failed to galvanize widespread political support for bringing the drug trade into the legal economy. The 1988 drug law satisfied some critics of national drug policy by giving greater emphasis, and funding, to the demand side of the problem. More money than ever before will go to treatment of addicts and to education programs aimed at preventing drug use over the next few years. But the 1988 law also calls for an escalation of the war on drugs, with additional spending on eradication, interdiction, and disruption of the retail trade. The Bush administration's new drug strategy promises more of the same. It cedes nothing to the supporters of legalization.

But both Congress and the Bush administration appear to have followed the will of most Americans. An ABC News poll conducted between August 30 and September 1, 1988, as the drug bill was making its way through the legislative process, indicated that nine out of ten Americans rejected the decriminalization of all illegal drugs. Only 25 percent supported the legalization of marijuana, and an even smaller minority said cocaine or heroin should be legal (7 percent and 6 percent respectively). Most agreed with Representative Rangel that legalization would lead to increased drug use.

So for now it's war. But down the road, legalization may be more seriously considered. Dr. David F. Musto, a professor of psychiatry at Yale University's Child Study Center and a well-known authority on drug abuse, believes the drug epidemic will soon run its course, just as an earlier cocaine epidemic came and went at the beginning of the twentieth century. Meanwhile, he says, the business of drugs is making a killing in the nation's inner cities. "We are headed toward a two-tiered drug-demand phenomenon in the United States," Musto says. "There is some evidence that drug use among people with rather clear, long-term personal and family goals is declining. In the inner city, on the other hand, the common complaint is that there is no hope and that the only people around who are accomplishing anything are the drug dealers."

Musto's view is supported by the findings of recent surveys. According to a survey of national high school seniors, drug use among 1988 high school graduates was lower than at any time since the University of Michigan began circulating its annual questionnaire in 1975.[12] Most important, the use of cocaine, including crack, was down for the second year in a row. From 1987 to 1988 the proportion of seniors who had tried cocaine at least once fell by one-fifth, to 15 percent. Of these, 40 percent had also smoked crack. But crack use too fell among high school seniors, with 5 percent reporting they had ever smoked the drug, down from 6 percent the year before (Figures 9-2 and 9-3).

Dr. Charles R. Schuster, director of the National Institute on Drug Abuse (NIDA), said that the findings show how effectively education can deter teenagers from drug use and prevent them from trying drugs in the first place. High school seniors, he said on releasing the data, "are hearing the messages about cocaine's dangers and are avoiding drug use in general. While crack cocaine is very available, seniors appear to be concerned about its addictive qualities and are less likely to try or continue use."

High school seniors also appear to be less likely to use any drugs. The 1988 survey found that fewer seniors had ever tried drugs. Moreover, 21 percent said they currently used any illicit drug, down from 25 percent of the 1987 graduating class. Marijuana topped the list of preferred substances, with almost half the seniors reporting they had used it at least once

Figure 9-2 Estimated Percentages of High School Seniors Who Reported Ever Having Used Drugs

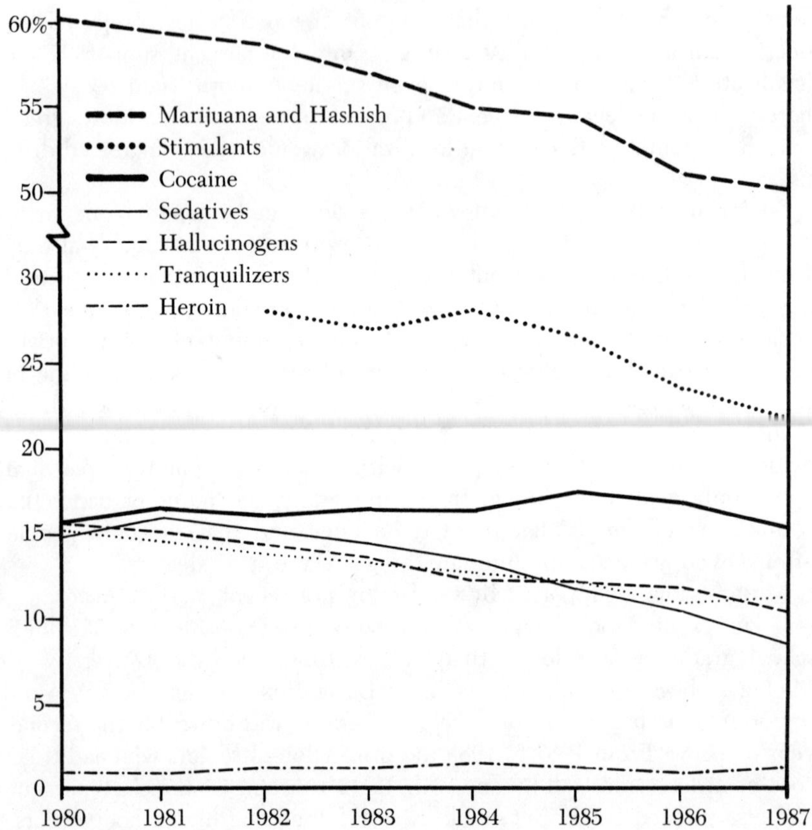

Source: U.S. Department of Health and Human Services, National Institute on Drug Abuse, *Monitoring the Future, 1987.*

and 18 percent saying they were current users. Stimulants and inhalants were the other most frequently used drugs.

But the high school survey is not an accurate barometer of trends in the drug-using population as a whole. High school seniors, after all, are the most successful members of their generation. True to Musto's prediction, drug use appears to be spreading among younger high school dropouts, who account for as much as half their age group in some large metropolitan areas. According to NIDA's National Household Survey on Drug Abuse of 1985, drug use among high school dropouts age nineteen to twenty-one was 67 percent higher than among their graduating peers. Most signifi-

Figure 9-3 Estimated Percentages of High School Students Who Reported Drug Use in Prior Thirty Days

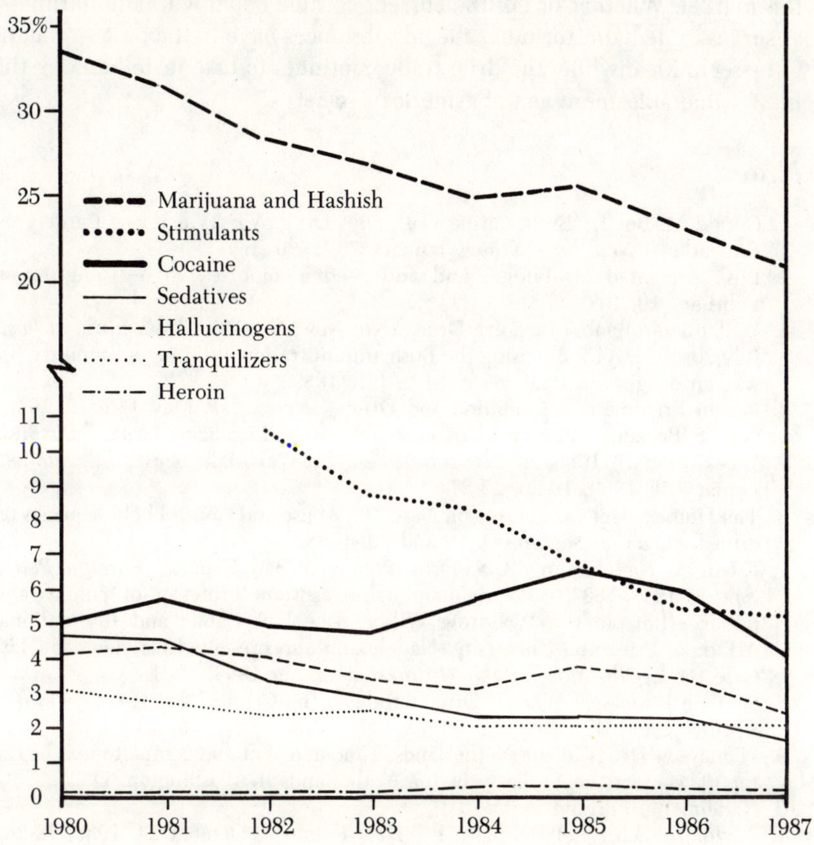

Source: U.S. Department of Health and Human Services, National Institute on Drug Abuse, *Monitoring the Future, 1987*.

cantly, the kinds of drugs these adolescent users turn to are the most dangerous and damaging ones, especially crack. The victims of cocaine are showing up in hospital emergency rooms in alarming numbers. NIDA's Drug Abuse Warning Network recorded more than 46,000 cases of cocaine-related emergencies and deaths in 1987, nearly twice as many as the year before.

These statistics provide further evidence that the real threat posed by the business of illegal drugs involves far more than the immediate physical dangers and economic disruption described in this volume. They suggest that the market for addictive illegal drugs such as crack is accelerating the division of American society into classes of haves and have-nots. The war on drugs has proved to be no match for the economic forces that sustain this market. Whether or not the current cocaine boom will fade in time—as surges in demand for other illegal substances have in the past—remains to be seen. Meanwhile, the drug trade continues to take its toll among the most vulnerable members of American society.

Notes

1. Gerald M. Boyd, "Bush, Citing Cost, Says Drug War Will Focus Largely on Education," *New York Times*, January 26, 1989, 1.
2. Bush presented his budget and addressed a joint session of Congress on February 10, 1989.
3. William von Raab, "Legalize Drugs? Not Now, Not Ever," *Washington Post*, July 20, 1988, A15. Accusing the Bush administration of failing to intensify the war on drugs, von Raab resigned in July 1989.
4. Milton Friedman, "Prohibition and Drugs," *Newsweek*, May 1, 1972, 104.
5. Gary S. Becker, "More People Are Saying 'Yes' to Legalizing Drugs," *Business Week*, June 27, 1988, 20. See also "Does This War Make Sense?" *Economist*, January 21, 1989, 19-20, 25-27.
6. The House Select Committee on Narcotics Abuse and Control held hearings on drug legalization September 16 and 29, 1988.
7. Ethan A. Nadelmann, "U.S. Drug Policy: A Bad Export," *Foreign Policy* (Spring 1988): 83-108. Nadelmann is an assistant professor of politics and public affairs in the Woodrow Wilson School of Public and International Affairs at Princeton University. Nadelmann also presented his views in "The Case for Legalization," *Public Interest* (Summer 1988): 3-31.
8. Stephen J. Morse, "War on Drugs Produces the Crime," *Los Angeles Times*, April 8, 1988, II7.
9. "Policy on Drugs in the Netherlands," undated. For the complete text of the report, contact the Embassy of the Netherlands in Washington, D.C.
10. Nadelmann, *Foreign Policy*, 107.
11. Taylor Branch, "Let Koop Do It," *New Republic*, October 24, 1988, 22-26.
12. University of Michigan, *Monitoring the Future: A Continuing Study of the Lifestyles and Values of Youth*, released February 28, 1989, by the National Institute on Drug Abuse (NIDA), which sponsored the survey.

Appendix Pharmacopeia of Illicit Drugs

Drug	Properties	Effects	Users	Price
Cocaine	A stimulant extracted from the leaves of the coca bush, cocaine is cultivated principally in Peru and exported mainly by Colombia. Cocaine is used in one of two forms. Cocaine hydrochloride, a white crystalline powder, is usually snorted, or inhaled through the nose, from a thin line of powder. Cocaine can also be dissolved in water and injected or reduced to free base, or crack, and smoked.	Euphoria is followed by depression as the drug's effects wane. Although physical dependency requiring daily use is uncommon with cocaine powder, scientists now believe that the psychological craving for the drug is produced by a true physiologic addiction.	Cocaine powder has long been a "socially acceptable" drug of the middle class. Crack is heavily used by inner-city poor, especially youth, but is moving into the suburbs.	Cocaine powder costs $25-$60 per one-half gram dose, whose effects can last for several hours. A quarter-gram dose of crack costs $10-$30 and will keep two or three people high for a half-hour to forty-five minutes.
Heroin	Heroin is a narcotic, or opiate, derived from the opium poppy. It is produced mainly in Southeast Asia, Southwest Asia, and Mexico. Heroin, a water-soluble powder, is sometimes sniffed but more often injected intravenously.	Upon absorption, heroin stimulates, then depresses, activity of the central nervous system. The initial rush, or surge of pleasure, is followed by a dream-like state that lasts from two to six hours. Heroin's addictive quality depends on the quantity, frequency, and duration of use. Strong addiction causes marked physical withdrawal symptoms.	Heroin users are mostly urban poor. Police say heroin addicts are mostly long-term users; there are few new recruits.	A quarter-gram dose costs about $20-$40. The effects at today's average purity levels last three or four hours.

(Appendix continues)

Appendix (continued)

Drug	Properties	Effects	Users	Price
Marijuana/ Hashish	Marijuana is a unique psychoactive drug consisting of the dried leaves and flowers of the cannabis plant. It can be smoked in a pipe or as a cigarette (a joint), or it can be ingested in food or drink. Hashish, the resin extract of cannabis, contains a higher concentration of THC, marijuana's active ingredient. In cake form, it is usually smoked in a pipe. Hashish oil is often mixed with tobacco and smoked.	There are variable degrees of intoxication. Some authorities say marijuana and hashish are non-addictive, while others claim they produce psychological dependency.	Marijuana is used by all social and ethnic groups.	One ounce of standard-grade marijuana costs $30-$250; high-grade sinsemilla costs $120-$300. One ounce of marijuana will make 28-30 joints, whose effects last several hours.
Hallucinogens (LSD, PCP)	LSD, or lysergic acid diethylamide, was originally synthesized in 1938 and used to treat psychosis and schizophrenia. As a drug of abuse, it is ingested. PCP, or phencyclidine, is a liquid that is put on tobacco, marijuana, or other plant material and then smoked. It was first synthesized as a veterinary anesthetic in the 1950s.	The effects of LSD range from dizziness and perceptions of bright lights and kaleidoscopic images to convulsions. PCP produces intoxication, loss of sensation of pain, and at times violent behavior. Stored in the body's fatty tissues, PCP can be released into the blood stream long after its initial effects have worn off.	LSD, a favorite of the "hippie" movement of the 1960s, is less widely used today. PCP, popular in Los Angeles and Washington, D.C., among lower-class and middle-class users, is unknown in many parts of the country.	LSD costs $3-$7 per 20-60 microgram dose, which lasts three to six hours. PCP-treated cigarettes, or "dipper," cost $25-$30 each. Effects vary and can recur.
Dilaudid	Dilaudid is synthetic morphine, used licitly to treat cancer symptoms and severe trauma such as gunshot wounds. As a painkiller, it is twice as strong as heroin.	Dilaudid is similar to heroin. In water-soluble pill form it is often ground up, mixed with water, and injected.	In Washington, D.C., lower-middle-class white adults abuse Dilaudid. It is also popular in Detroit, Philadelphia, and New Orleans.	One 4-milligram dose costs $35-$40 and the effects last several hours. Smaller doses are also sold.

Index